# The World's Best Dirty Stories

D0334761

# The World's Best Dirty Stories

A full and fearless account of
the campaigns of Colonel Castarse

John Gurney

Illustrated by Nigel Gurney

ANGUS
& ROBERTSON
PUBLISHERS

ANGUS & ROBERTSON PUBLISHERS

Unit 4, Eden Park, 31 Waterloo Road,
North Ryde, NSW, Australia 2113, and
16 Golden Square, London W1R 4BN,
United Kingdom

First published as The Campaigns of
Colonel Castarse in 1983
This edition first published in Australia
by Angus & Robertson Publishers and in
the United Kingdom by Angus & Robertson
UK in 1984
Reprinted 1985, 1986 (twice)

National Library of Australia
Cataloguing-in-publication data.

Gurney, John, 1929–
    The world's best dirty stories.

    Previously published as:
    The campaigns of Colonel Castarse.
    London; Sydney: Angus & Robertson, 1983.
    ISBN 0 207 15071 0.

    I. Australian wit and humour.
    I. Gurney, Nigel.
    II. Gurney, John, 1929–
    Campaigns of Colonel Castarse.
    III. Title. IV. Title:
    Campaigns of Colonel Castarse.
A828'.307

Typeset in 11pt Paladium by
Setrite Typesetters, Hong Kong

Printed in Great Britain by
Hazell Watson & Viney Limited

*This volume is gratefully dedicated to all those merry souls who have brightened our lives from time to time by sharing with us tales of the exploits of that redoubtable warrior, Colonel Reginald Castarse. We hope that readers knowing episodes we have not included will be kind enough to make them known to us.*

# CONTENTS

# INTRODUCTION

Down through the years, in widely separate places, wherever fellows join in a convivial glass and tell humorous yarns, sooner or later someone will mention the Colonel. Many indeed are the stories told about him, and the character that emerges from them is remarkably consistent. Although many believe he was a legendary figure, it is our belief that he did exist. And so we have compiled this collection of his exploits.

Although it is as comprehensive as we could make it, there are no doubt episodes we have missed. There is, for example, no material available about his early career in the British Army before he became a Colonel.

The stories are set out in what would seem to be a logical sequence, according to the Colonel's age, the campaigns he took part in, and so on, but we cannot claim that they are in exact chronological order so as to make up an accurate biography.

And so we introduce you to the Colonel as we first heard of him some thirty years ago, a young officer embarking on a distinguished career.

# PRELIMINARY SKIRMISHING

As a young man Reginald Castarse was well schooled in all the social graces. He could order dinner and select wine from a menu in French. He dressed in good taste without appearing too natty. He played above average golf and tennis, and could ride to hounds. But what he enjoyed most of all was ballroom dancing.

On one occasion he attended a dance at the Deaf and Dumb Institute. A band was playing and he was amazed that the inmates were able to feel the vibrations through the floor and so enjoy this social grace as fully as any hearing person. He decided that it would be good experience to have a dance with one of the girls.

There was a very attractive blonde seated half-way along the room. He approached her and made gestures inviting her to dance. She rose and smiled.

She was really a very good dancer, and after the set concluded he invited her in the same way for another. This continued until supper, when he made gestures for drinking tea, and the two linked arms and made their way towards the supper room.

As they did so a burly young man accosted the young lady

and said, "What's this? I thought you were going to have supper with me."

The girl replied, "I was too. Only, I can't seem to get rid of this deaf and dumb chap."

On another occasion the Colonel was dancing with a young American girl whose necklace became unfastened and slipped down the back of her dress. She asked him to retrieve the jewellery for her. He was very embarrassed, but wishing to comply with her request, he reached cautiously down the back of her gown.

"I'm terribly sorry," he said, "but I can't seem to reach it."

"Try further down," she said.

At this point, he became aware that he was being watched by everyone in the room.

"I say," he whispered, "I feel a perfect ass."

"Never mind that," she replied. "Just get the necklace."

At the Regimental Ball, young Castarse's eye was taken by an attractive young woman sitting to one side with a rug over her lap. He approached her and gave her his most winning smile.

"May I have the pleasure of this dance, and all that?"

The girl smiled sadly. "I'd love to dance with you, Colonel, really I would, but, you see, I can't. I have no legs. That's why I have this rug over my lap."

"Oh, I say! I'm frightfully sorry, I've really embarrassed you. I'm no gentleman. Do you mind if I sit and talk with you?"

"Please do."

Young Castarse took a seat beside the young lady and they had quite a long conversation. She was a charming companion, and he spent the entire evening with her.

After the ball, he offered to drive her home. She accepted, and he carried her outside and installed her in his MG. Following her directions, her was soon parked opposite her front gate.

After brief preliminaries, they were soon kissing and embracing passionately. But after a time the Colonel sat back dejected.

"I say, I'm awfully sorry. I'm no gentleman. First I

embarrass you at the Regimentall Ball, then I monopolise you for the whole evening, and here I am taking liberties like this when I hardly know you. I'm no gentleman at all."

"Don't you feel that way, Colonel. I've enjoyed having your company during the evening. If you hadn't stayed with me I might have had no one to talk with all night. And as for taking liberties as you put it, you mustn't think such a thing. You don't suppose that having no legs stops me from having normal feelings, do you?"

She gave him a lingering kiss.

"Well actually, you know, what I really want to do is make love to you properly, but there's no room in this little car, and I don't quite know how we might manage."

"If you reach behind my back, between my shoulders, you will find a large hook, held in place by a strap. If you carry me over to the front fence, and slip the hook over the top rail, it might just work the trick."

The experiment was a complete success, and the deed soon accomplished, but immediately afterwards Castarse was again overcome with remorse.

"I say, I feel awful about this, really I do. I'm no gentleman at all, taking advantage of you in this way. Let me help you inside."

After he had carried her into the house and settled her into an armchair, he again apologised, "I don't know what you must think of me after the way I've behaved. I'm no gentleman at all."

"Oh but you are a gentleman," she said earnestly. "All the others used to leave me hanging on the front fence."

With the passage of time he became much more experienced, and streamlined his approach drastically.

The Colonel was dancing one evening with a sweet young thing and as they circled the floor he murmured to her, "I say, Miss, do you fuck?"

The unfortunate girl blushed and pretended not to hear.

The Colonel asked her a second time, "I say, Miss, do you fuck?"

Feeling decidedly uncomfortable, the poor girl still said

nothing but the Colonel asked her a third time, "I say, Miss, do you fuck?"

Whereupon the girl said to the Colonel, "Do you ask that question of every girl you dance with?"

The Colonel replied, "I should say so. Yes. Very definitely."

"You must get an awful lot of knock-backs," she observed.

"Oh I do. I do," said the Colonel. "But I also get an awful lot of fucks."

After a dinner party one evening, the Colonel was driving a young woman home. When he put his hand on her knee she said to him, "I only have two words to say to you. Filthy beast."

The Colonel drove on in silence and when he stopped outside her home he said to her, "I only have two words to say to you. Let go."

An end came to all this with an afternoon tea given by Lady Nettlefield. After various other entertainments the guests fell to playing at riddles.

When it was his turn, the Colonel was asked, "What part of the human body is surrounded by hair, is capable of enlarging to ten times its normal size, and gets hot and wet when you poke your finger in it?"

The Colonel did not hesitate. "A cunt," he replied.

There was a stunned silence. The answer should have been the pupil of the eye. The hostess swept from the room. The other guests avoided him. No one would speak to him.

The Colonel was disgraced. News of his dreadful behaviour spread throughout social circles. To escape, he applied for a posting overseas and left England soon afterwards.

As luck would have it, many years later, when he returned home flushed with victory and famous for his exploits at the Khyber Pass and other places, he was feted and lionised by many of the same people who had shunned him before. He was even guest of honour at an afternoon tea given by Lady Nettlefield. After a time the guests again began playing at riddles. The Colonel's turn came.

"What part of the human body is surrounded by hair, is capable of enlarging to ten times its normal size, and gets hot and wet when you poke your finger in it?" he was asked.

The Colonel replied stubbornly, "I don't care what you say. The answer's still a cunt."

During the war in Egypt, the guests at Shepheard's Hotel, Cairo, were awakened one night by a loud screaming and stamping in the passageway. True to the form of all hotel guests, they all peered out of their doors just in time to catch sight of a young damsel in extreme negligée, fleeing wildly down the passage from a young man who was, to put it bluntly, nude.

Next morning it transpired that the impetuous Romeo was a high-ranking British officer named Castarse, and that he was likely not only to be court-martialled and lose his rank, but also face a suit for civil damages since the young lady belonged to an important local family.

However, the Castarse family was not without resources and engaged the services of an eminent KC to conduct the defence. It was due to an astute move on the part of this gentleman that Castarse was able not only to avoid the civil action, but also retain his rank.

The defence counsel merely quoted a paragraph in the Army Manual which states:

"It is not compulsory for an Officer of the British Army to wear full uniform at all times, provided that he is suitably garbed for the sport in which he is engaged."

When the Colonel was on duty in Cairo, the hotel at which he was staying was some distance from headquarters. Petrol was extremely scarce, so the Colonel bought himself a camel, on which he used to ride to and from headquarters every day.

In the Officers' Club one evening, Featherstonwhore remarked to the Colonel what a fine beast his camel was.

"She, you mean," replied the Colonel, "she's a female, don't you know."

"Oh, not at all, Colonel," said Featherstonwhore, "he's definitely a male."

"Of course she's a female," said the Colonel. "Only this morning as I was riding past the bazaar I heard one of those vulgar Australian soldiers call out, 'Hey, look at the big cunt on that camel'."

Carruthers paid his money for a session with an Egyptian whore in Cairo. After caressing his prick for several minutes until he had a fine erection, the girl then poured over it two tablespoons of honey, half a cup of whipped cream, sprinkled it with chopped walnuts and put a maraschino cherry on top.

Carruthers was fascinated.

"Look here. What's all this in aid of?"

"Now I am going to suck it off."

"No you're not. You leave it alone. I'm going to suck it off myself."

The Colonel was in Cairo and had to travel to Damascus within three weeks to conclude an important matter. He went to the camel market and sought out Ben Ali who had a reputation for being an honest dealer.

"I want the best, most reliable beast you have," he told Ben Ali. "I must be in Damascus within three weeks and I don't want to be let down. The price is not important."

"See this fellow here," said Ben Ali. "He's the best beast in Cairo. He will get you there. But be sure to give him plenty to drink before you start."

"How much?" asked the Colonel.

"Thirty thousand piastres."

The camel changed hands.

Before setting out the Colonel took the camel to a trough where the beast drank and drank until the Colonel thought he would never stop. At last he finished and they set forth.

They hadn't been travelling more than a week when the camel, completely without warning, collapsed to the sand. When the Colonel examined him he proved to be quite dead. With a few kind words to say about Ben Ali, the Colonel gathered his belongings and was lucky enough to get a lift to Damascus in a caravan in time to fulfil his mission. He then headed back to Cairo.

On his arrival he could hardly wait to see Ben Ali. He went to the camel market and found him.

"Fine sort of a rogue you turned out to be, Ben Ali," said the Colonel.

"Why, Colonel, what do you mean?" protested Ben Ali.

"That camel you sold me. You said he was the best in Cairo."

"Oh he was. He was. What happened?"

"We only travelled for a week and he fell down dead."

"I can't understand it," said Ben Ali. He was a fine beast. Did you give him plenty to drink before you started?"

"Of course I did."

"And did you brick him?"

"Brick him? What do you mean?"

"Ah. Well, Colonel, when the camel is having his big drink before you set out, you have these two bricks ready, and when he is just about to stop drinking, you bang his balls

8

between the bricks as hard as you can and he sucks in enough water to last for another two weeks."

While the Colonel was in the Middle East, he became very friendly with a sheikh who one day showed him round his palace. After they had seen the great hall, the banquet room, the harem, the kitchen and the stables, the sheikh asked him whether he might like to see the room where they made the eunuchs.

"Most certainly," replied the Colonel. "By all means."

The sheikh took him down a stone staircase and into a room with a bare stone floor. Its only furnishings were two parallel iron bars about the thickness of broomsticks that ran from one side of the room to the other about two inches apart and four feet off the floor. On the floor below were two bricks.

The Colonel looked for a time and then admitted, "I'm afraid I don't understand."

The sheikh explained that the selected candidate was seated on the two bars so that his testicles hung down between the bars. A man standing behind him then banged them firmly between the two bricks.

The Colonel shuddered. "I say, that must be awfully painful," he remarked.

"Oh it is," replied the sheikh, "especially when you get your thumb caught between the bricks."

The Colonel had been stationed in the desert for some weeks and the strain was becoming too much for him. He took Featherstonwhore aside and said to him, "I say, old boy, what do you do when you want a bit of sexual excitement?"

"No trouble, Colonel. You just use the camels."

The Colonel was aghast at the suggestion and went on for many weeks until at last he could stand it no longer.

Taking a stepladder down to the camel compound he led one of the female camels into a corner and, positioning the ladder carefully, climbed up. After removing his trousers, he was having some difficulty in keeping the beast still, when who should walk into the compound but Featherstonwhore.

"Good Lord, Colonel. What are you doing up there?"

9

"I'm trying to screw this damned camel."

"What on earth for?"

"Well you told me, when I wanted a bit of sexual excitement to use the camels."

"Well of course, dear boy, you use the camels to ride into the village. It's less than twenty miles away."

At an even more remote outpost the Colonel was amazed one day, after weeks of relative inactivity, to see everyone in the camp running wildly into the desert yelling, "The camels are coming. The camels are coming."

Stopping one of the men he asked, "What's the hurry?"

The man replied, "Well, sir, you've got to be early to get yourself a good-looking camel."

The troopship was crossing the Indian Ocean and the Colonel was randy as hell. He had his eye on the ship's nurse, who was shapely but prudish. Although it took a whole week to get the top button undone, he persisted. With only two more weeks to go, he thought seriously of taking the bastion by storm and planting his standard between the ramparts, but his nerve failed.

As luck would have it, the ship was torpedoed and while the captain was giving emergency orders, the Colonel appeared on the bridge and asked, "Is the ship sinking?"

"Clear off. I'm busy," replied the captain. "What's the matter? Are you scared?"

"Not at all, sir, but if we're going to sink I intend to use the last five minutes making that bitch's mind up for her."

The vessel finally limped into port in England, and the Colonel was at last able to enjoy a spell of leave. One Monday morning he stormed into the local chemist shop, and demanded to see the proprietor.

"Look here," the Colonel said, "Friday evening I came in here and bought a gross of condoms. Then when I open them up, I find there's only ten dozen."

"Naturally, we will replace the missing items," said the chemist smoothly. "Hope your weekend wasn't spoiled, sir."

The Colonel decided to use some of the time he had available for a short holiday in the South of France. The day of his arrival in France was fine and warm. He made his way to the beach and stretched out in the sun. After a time he became aware of an attractive blonde, a short distance away, looking at him.

She smiled.

He smiled in return.

She walked over to him and said, "Are you buying?"

"Oh, well. I might as well."

The blonde visited his room a number of times during his stay.

The following summer, the Colonel again made for the South of France. First morning on the beach, who should he see but the same blonde. She smiled and walked over to him.

"Are you buying?"

The Colonel was surly. "What are you selling this year? Leprosy?"

The Colonel prided himself on his French and used it in Paris whenever possible. One day he ordered a glass of wine. When the waiter brought it, the Colonel found a dead fly floating in it upside down. He called the waiter back.

"*Regardez. Dans mon vin. Le mouche.*"

"Not *le mouche, monsieur. La mouche,*" replied the waiter.

"My word," exclaimed the Colonel. "I must say you've got better eyesight than I have."

The Colonel went into a bar in Madrid not far from the bull-ring. Inside he found that all the walls were decorated with the heads of the beasts that had been killed in the arena.

He was so impressed by them that when the waiter brought his drink, he remarked, "Jove. These bulls' heads are huge. They're like small elephants' heads."

The waiter set down the drink and solemnly pointed to one large head.

"That one killed my grandfather."

"In the bullring?"

"No. He was sitting under it when it fell off the wall."

# PITCHED BATTLE

As the Colonel's progress appeared to be a little wild, even for the Castarse family, they decided that what he most needed to settle him down was a good marriage. A match was arranged with a young woman of good family. The fact that the Colonel hardly knew her was scarcely taken into account.

On the Colonel's wedding night, his bride appeared from her dressing room wearing a floor-length transparent nightie and pulling on a pair of shoulder-length white kid gloves.

"I say, my love, you look perfectly ravishing, really you do, but what are the long gloves for?"

"Well," she said, "I believe you're expected to handle the filthy thing."

A week after their wedding, the Colonel's bride visited the doctor for some further sex education.

"Doctor," she said, "that long thing hanging down between my husband's legs. What is it called?"

"That, my dear, is his penis."

"And what about the red knob on the end of it?"

"That is known as the tip or glans."

"Yes, well. About fourteen inches back from that are two round things hanging down. What are they?"

"Well, I don't know about your husband, but on me they'd be haemorrhoids."

When their honeymoon was over, the Colonel brought his bride back to the village and took her the last three miles to his house in an old wooden cart drawn by a donkey. At first she thought this was most romantic but then the donkey stopped for no reason. When the beast did not respond to his urgings, the Colonel stepped out of the cart and dealt the donkey a severe blow over the head with a block of wood.

"That's one," he said, and resumed his place in the cart.

The donkey and cart moved on for another mile or so, and then the donkey stopped again. Once more the Colonel urged the beast on, to no avail, and finally resorted to another blow over the head with the block of wood.

"That's two," he said.

He climbed in and they moved off. When they had almost reached the house, the donkey stopped a third time. More urging. No result.

"That's three," said the Colonel, and taking a rifle from the cart he blew the donkey's brains out.

This was too much for his bride, who berated him. "You cruel beast," she exclaimed. "Fancy knocking the poor brute about like that and then expecting him to do as you tell him! And then to shoot him in cold blood! Why that donkey must have been worth thirty pounds if he was worth a penny. You're not only a cruel beast, you're an extravagant fool."

"That's one," the Colonel said.

Very early in their marriage, the Colonel's bride was fondling his penis and asked him, "Darling, didn't you say you were the only man who had one of these?"

"Yes, of course, my dear. Why?"

"Well I just found out today that the footman, George, has one too."

"Yes. Well. Ah, that's because I used to have a spare, you know, and I gave it to him."

"Well, you were a bit silly," she said. "You gave the best one away."

The barber shop was crowded. As he finished cutting the Colonel's hair, the barber asked, "Shall I spray a little scent on it, sir?"

"Good Lord no," the Colonel replied. "If I went home plastered with that stuff, my wife would say I smelled like a brothel."

Just then a private in the next chair was asked the same question.

"Go ahead," he declared loudly. "Spray on as much as you like. My wife don't know what a brothel smells like."

While visiting the patients in the local hospital, the Colonel's wife noticed that one patient had his private parts heavily bandaged.

"Did you break the bone in it?" she asked the man.

"Bone? Bone? How long have you and the Colonel been married?"

"Four months."

"Well, I takes my hat off to the Colonel."

Soon after, the Colonel was posted to the Far East. When he had been there for some time, his wife came to visit him at his station.

The first morning his Chinese valet woke her by slapping her on the buttocks, saying, "All light, Missy, time for bleakfast, then you go home."

To make amends for this unfortunate incident, the Colonel purchased from a jeweller in Hong Kong a jade pendant, inscribed with Chinese characters worked in gold. This he sent, not to his wife, but to his wife's mother, who was delighted.

She wore the pendant everywhere and showed it to all her friends, saying, "You see this? My son-in-law gave me this. Isn't it lovely?"

One evening she was a guest at an ambassadorial function

and was introduced to the Chinese ambassador. She at once showed him the pendant.

"You see this? My son-in-law gave it to me."

"Ah, so. Yes. Very nice."

"Can you read it?"

"Ah so. Yes. Very nice."

"Well, what does the Chinese writing say?"

"It say 'Government of Hong Kong. Licensed Prostitute, Second Class'."

One day the Colonel had a call from a friend in another regiment. "I say, Castarse, this Major Chumley that's coming over to you on transfer from my regiment. I feel I ought to warn you. He's an inveterate gambler. Nothing we've been able to do has cured him. See what you can do, old chap."

During his initial interview with Chumley the Colonel was startled by the question: "I say, Colonel, do you suffer badly from piles?"

The Colonel replied that he didn't have piles at all.

"Oh I'm sure you're quite mistaken, Colonel. In fact I'd be prepared to bet you five hundred pounds about it."

Thinking this was a good chance to cure Chumley of his obsession with gambling, the Colonel accepted the bet. Of course it was necessary for Chumley to examine the Colonel to satisfy himself, but in the end he paid up the five hundred pounds.

The Colonel was delighted and immediately rang up his old friend.

"I've cured Chumley of gambling once and for all," he told him, and recounted the events of the initial interview.

"Oh no!" his friend replied. "He bet all of us a thousand pounds that he'd have his finger up your arse within twenty-four hours of joining your regiment."

The Chinese cook in the Officers' Mess was very badly treated by the officers, who tied knots in his queue, put frogs in his slippers and generally teased him unmercifully. Eventually they had a change of heart and assured him that they would not torment him any more. The Chinese was sceptical.

"No kickee?"

"No kickee," he was assured.

"No knottee in hair?"

"No more knots in your hair, John."

"Hokay. Me no pissee in coffee any more!"

It was in India that Colonel Castarse received word that young Ffanshawe was being transferred to the Colonel's regiment. The lad had splendid references and an excellent record, and, when he arrived, the Colonel welcomed him effusively.

"Glad to have you with us, dear boy. I know you're going to like it here. Such a lot of things to do."

"Oh yes, Colonel. I've been looking forward to it. Defending the Khyber Pass. Fighting the Sikhs and Gurkhas. It must be wonderful."

"No, no, lad. That sort of thing is all in the past now. The natives are very well behaved. We have other activities now. A full programme in fact. Now tomorrow is Tuesday. Tuesday we have polo. You play polo, of course?"

"Actually no, I don't."

"Hmm. Well, Wednesday we have bridge. Lot of fun to be had on Wednesdays."

"I'm afraid I don't play bridge either, sir."

"I see. Well, you'll enjoy Thursdays anyway. Thursday is more or less a social day. One big party. Lots of wife-swapping and carry-on. You'll like Thursdays."

"Oh, sir, I couldn't take part in anything like that."

"Why not? Are you some kind of homosexual or something?"

"Oh no, sir. Certainly not."

"Oh. Well I'm afraid you won't enjoy Fridays much either."

The Colonel was briefing the new arrivals in India about the local conditions.

"Now, about snakes. The bite from a cobra can be deadly if not treated, but with proper treatment is not really dangerous at all. If it bites you, simply make two cross cuts in the bite and suck out the poison."

"But, sir! What if it bites you on the arse?"

"Then that's when you find out who your real friends are."

The men at the regimental dinner were all very drunk, including the Colonel. He came back from the men's room with his fly undone and as he sat down Featherstonwhore exclaimed, "I say Colonel, there was a big snake on that chair when you sat down."

"Was there?"

"Yes. A great big snake on your chair. I can see the head there now. I'll kill it."

He seized a champagne bottle and brought it crashing down.

The Colonel winced.

"Hit it again. It just bit me."

At the dinner the Colonel ate, drank and smoked to excess. Afterwards he was sick down the front of his mess jacket.

The next morning, he said to his batman, "Coming home from the dinner last night some bounder was tight and blundered into me. He was sick all down the front of my mess jacket, the cad. You might clean it up, and when you bring it back remind me to give that man fourteen days, will you?"

The next day the batman returned the clothes cleaned and pressed, and said, "If I were you, sir, I'd make it twenty-eight days. The dirty devil's shit in your trousers as well."

At last he was relieved of duty in the Orient and returned to England with anticipation.

One evening he was entertaining some American officers to dinner at his home. One of the guests showed particularly bad form by constantly comparing things in England unfavourably with the way things were "back home in the States".

After dinner, James approached the American and asked, "How do you like your coffee, sir?"

"I like my coffee like I like my women — hot and strong."

"White — or black?"

James was showing one American guest through the gallery full of ancestral portraits. He explained that this was Lord Henry who fought at the Armada, that this was Lord Humphrey who escaped with Bonnie Prince Charlie in women's clothes. So they went on until James stopped before the largest portrait.

"And this is Sir Gyles, the founder of the family."

"And what did he do?" asked the American.

"He was the founder of the family."

"Yes, but what did he do in the daytime?"

Early in World War II in France, a Cameronian, McPherson, was swimming in a stream near the Maginot Line. He stepped out on the bank, stood naked for a moment, then suddenly fell down unconscious. He came to in the base hospital, where the doctor said, "A sniper has shot you and hit both testicles. They're blown off so cleanly there's nothing for me to do except sew up the wound."

McPherson scratched his head and said, "It was sure lucky for me, doctor. If I hadna been thinkin' of me wife's maiden sister at the time, I'd ha' lost me gun too."

The Colonel and twenty of his men were invited by an old lady to a cocktail party, but were surprised to be served lemonade and biscuits. When each man had had about ten biscuits, one single biscuit remained in the dish. The old lady said, "Just one left, boys. What shall we do with it?"

The Colonel stood up immediately and said, "The man that answers that question will be given fourteen days confined to barracks."

The Colonel's wife was dismissing her maid and took the opportunity to make some caustic remarks about the girl's incompetence as a cook, a housekeeper and general help.

The girl was stung by this angry sarcasm and flared back, "The Colonel, Madam, considers me a much better cook and housekeeper than you."

"Indeed," scoffed the Colonel's wife.

"Yes, and furthermore, I'm a better lover than you are, too."

"I suppose that's another thing the Colonel told you."

"No, the chauffeur told me that."

The Colonel's wife regularly visited the district military hospital. She talked to the patients and offered each of them a slice of sponge cake which she herself had made. Most of the men were tolerant of this and she usually came away convinced that her visit had cheered up the patients.

One morning she had completed her rounds and saw the matron before she left.

"I didn't know you had any Russian soldiers in this hospital," she said.

"We don't," replied the matron.

"That's strange. I went up to one man at the end of Ward B to give him some sponge cake, and when I asked him what his name was he said 'Opitchabitch'."

One of the soldiers in hospital had his head swathed in bandages and was being given his morning coffee rectally through a tube. Suddenly the man began to wave his arms and grunt through his bandages.

"What's the matter?" asked the nurse. "Is it too hot?"

"Mmmmno-no-no," came the muffled response. "Too much sugar."

During World War II the Colonel arranged for an old ship's carpenter to lecture a group of army officers on technical details to prepare for the invasion of France. His talk was forever being interrupted when he pronounced the names of trees as 'helm' and 'hash'. A very la-di-da voice from one of the younger officers would correct him, "You mean elm and ash, of course, don't you?"

At last, the old carpenter lost his patience. He said, "Now 'ere we 'ave the hoak."

"You mean oak, of course."

"Of coss. It is the very finest wood to use for pounding piles into piers. And for the benefit of our young friend 'ere, I don't mean pushin' 'emmorhoids hup the harses or hanuses of the haristocracy."

The Colonel was making an extremely rough sea voyage and gallantly gave up his cabin to a sick old woman in steerage class. He reported the incident to his wife by telegram:

"Dreadful stormy passage. Deathly sick all the way. Finally gave berth to an old woman."

The Admiral had been taking part in naval exercises. After they were over he was having a few drinks with two Admirals, one was Australian and the other was an American.

The conversation turned to courage. Naturally, each of the three was convinced that his own men showed the most.

Eventually the Admiral took the American and the Australian up on deck.

"I'll show you what real courage is. Willoughby!" he called.

Far above them from the crow's nest came the reply, "Aye, aye, sir."

"Willoughby! Jump!"

"Aye, aye, sir!"

Without a moment's hesitation the rating jumped from the crow's nest, still saluting. He landed on the deck. He was quite dead.

The Admiral said, "What do you think of that for courage, eh?"

By way of reply the American took them to his own flagship. "Vandersluce!" he called.

"Aye, aye, sir!"

"Vandersluce! Jump!"

"Aye, aye, sir!"

Still saluting, the rating jumped from the crow's nest and landed on the deck at their feet, quite dead.

"There you are," said the American. "There's courage for you."

"You two've got a lot to learn about courage," said the Australian. "Come with me."

He took them to the Australian flagship. On the deck he called up to the crow's nest, "Are you there, Mulga?"

"Aye, aye, sir."

"Mulga! Jump!"

"Jump? You must be pissed again, you silly old bastard. Go and get fucked."

"There," said the Australian Admiral to the other two. "That's what I call real guts."

In Canada the Colonel was visiting the headquarters of the Royal Canadian Northwest Mounted Police. It was explained to him that as well as having certain formal qualifications, new recruits were expected to pass an unofficial initiation test. In one night the candidate had to drink two bottles of whisky, shoot a grizzly bear, and make love to an Eskimo woman. The Colonel didn't think this would be too difficult, and volunteered to take the test himself that very night.

After he had drunk the two bottles of whisky, he disappeared into the darkness. He was gone for some time.

He finally reappeared after two hours — a mass of blood and scratches.

"What happened, Colonel?" he was asked.

"Never mind that," he replied. "Just show me where this Eskimo woman is that I have to shoot."

After this harrowing experience, the Colonel decided to go on a hunting expedition in the northern woods. His travel agent was asked to arrange a de luxe trip. The agent explained to the Colonel that the key to the success of the expedition was the French-Canadian guide, Pierre, who would paddle the canoe, bait the fish-hooks, build the fire, cook the food and prepare the eiderdown sleeping bag for the Colonel. When they reached the hunting grounds, the Colonel was to load his gun while Pierre made the sound of the female moose in heat, "Be-ee-eep! Br-e-e-e-eep!" And from far away would come the reply of the male moose, "Bo-o-oop! Br-o-o-ooop!" It would come closer and closer, until finally, when the bull-moose was close enough, all the Colonel had to do was fire the gun.

"But what if I miss?" asked the Colonel nervously.

"Oh well, in that case," said the agent, "Pierre gets fucked."

The Colonel was told in the southern mountains of a raccoon hunter who was the local champion.

"No one can touch him for hunting raccoons," the Colonel was told. "He has his own style."

The champion hunter offered to take the Colonel out with him on a hunt, to show him how he did it. No guns were taken by the champion, who assured the Colonel that he would not need a gun either, but the Colonel took one along anyhow.

The secret of the hunter's art was his marvellously trained dog, Blue, who sniffed out the raccoons and chased them up a tree. The hunter would then shake the tree until the raccoon fell out, whereupon Blue seized the raccoon and fucked it to death.

At the third try, a particularly big raccoon was treed, and the hunter could not get it down by shaking the tree. He climbed the tree himself to poke it down, but the raccoon fought back and bit the hunter savagely, causing him to fall out of the tree.

As he fell he screamed to the Colonel, "Shoot Blue! Shoot Blue!"

In Australia, the Colonel was attending a public lecture by a visiting speaker from the United States. The speaker was attacking the White Australia Policy.

"You Australians shouldn't be keeping out migrants from other countries. You should be encouraging them to come here. Why, in my veins there flows the blood of Italians, French, Norwegians, Russians, Polish, Spanish, Irish and Greek as well as Red Indian."

In the silence, the Colonel's voice could be heard, "Jove, his mother must've been a sporting sort, what?"

While in Australia the Colonel went to a race meeting and noticed a trainer acting suspiciously. He appeared to be slipping a horse something he took to be dope. The Colonel approached the trainer and asked him about it.

"Dope?" said the trainer. "Certainly not. Just sugar. Look, I'll eat a piece myself. Here. You have one too."

Both men ate the sugar. The Colonel apologised and went away.

Soon afterwards the trainer was giving the jockey his riding instructions — what position to take up and hold, when to make his run, and so on. He finished up by saying, "Just hang on and don't worry about a thing. If anything passes you it will only be the Colonel or me."

The Colonel and his wife had a suite in one of London's modern new hotels and were to attend a dinner dance in the ballroom that evening. While his wife went out in the afternoon to have her hair done, the Colonel went down to the lounge to have a few brandies to pass the time. It was here that he was approached by a call girl.

"Are you looking for a woman?"

"Oh, well. I'm always interested in whatever's going. What's it worth?"

"What do you think's a fair thing?"

"I don't know. A couple of quid, I suppose."

She laughed. "Huh! You don't get much these days for a couple of quid," she said and walked off.

In due course the Colonel returned to the suite and brought his wife, suitably coiffed, down to the ballroom for the dinner dance.

When the music started and a few couples began moving on to the floor, the Colonel led his wife out for a dance.

Soon the Colonel found himself confronted by the girl he had spoken to in the lounge. She looked his wife up and down and then said to the Colonel, "What did I tell you? You don't get much these days for a couple of quid."

Suspicious of his wife, the Colonel hired a detective agency to keep track of her while he was away on a trip. The agency used all its technical facilities on the assignment.

When the Colonel returned from his trip he went to the agency's headquarters, where he saw still and movie pictures and tape recordings.

It was true. His wife was having an affair — and with one of his friends. The evidence was conclusive — glamorous nights at parties, secret assignations at luxury hotels, nude bathing, whispered endearments, intimate laughter.

"I can't believe it," said the Colonel.

"About your friend's involvement?"

"No, I could believe anything of him," he said sadly. "I just can't believe that my wife could be that much fun."

Ponsonby complained to the manager of an hotel where he was staying about the dinner he had been served.

"There was a hair in the spaghetti. It's just not good enough. I'm not paying for it."

Later the manager came across Ponsonby when he had his head between the legs of one of the cocktail waitresses.

"Well, Mr Ponsonby! I see you don't mind having hair in your mouth now."

"No, I don't," Ponsonby replied, "but if I find any spaghetti down here, I'm not paying for this either."

The Colonel and his wife were Chief Patrons of the Agricultural Show, and after the official opening, dutifully walked around looking at the exhibits and mixing with the tenants and peasantry.

The Colonel lingered so long in the refreshment tent that his wife wandered off to admire the prize bull. Never was a male animal so splendidly equipped.

"My word. That's a fine beast you have there, Giles," she said to the yokel in charge.

"Yes Mum. 'E be champion, and father o' champions."

"Tell me about him."

"Well, Mum, this yere bull stood to stud three 'undred times last year."

"Indeed? Be a good fellow, Giles. Go over to the Colonel, and tell him there's a bull here that went to stud three hundred times in one year, will you?"

Giles made his way over to the Colonel and gave him the message.

"Very interesting," observed the Colonel. "Always the same cow, I suppose?"

"No indeed, sir. Three 'undred different cows."

"I see. Go and tell my wife that, too, will you?"

When the Colonel's wife learned that he had taken a mistress, she demanded, "Does this mean that you've had enough of me?"

"No, my dear," he replied coolly. "It means that I haven't had enough of you."

The Colonel visited the local GP for a check-up. The nurse asked him to undress — the doctor would be in shortly to examine him. When she came back with the doctor, she was surprised to see a corset on top of his pile of underwear.

"Why, Colonel. I didn't know you had back trouble."

"Well, actually, my dear, I don't. I've been wearing a corset ever since my wife found one in the glove box of my car."

The Colonel's wife found him in bed with a long-haired lovely, she was furious and picked up a heavy ashtray, ready to launch it at him.

"She's just a poor hitch-hiker I picked up on the highway," the Colonel tried to explain. "She was hungry, so I brought her home and fed her. Then I saw her sandals were worn out, so I gave her that old pair you haven't worn for at least ten years. Then I noticed her shirt was torn, so I gave her an old blouse you haven't looked at for ages. And her jeans were all patched, so I gave her an old pair of slacks you never wear.

"But as she was getting ready to leave, she asked me, 'Is there anything else your wife doesn't use?'"

The Colonel's friend, Ponsonby, picked up an old whore who took him up to her room. Just as he was getting started a big Alsatian dog walked in through the door.

"Outside, Rover," commanded the whore. "You had yours this morning."

Hearing this, Ponsonby at once got off the bed and began to get dressed.

"I've ridden after hounds before," he complained, "but I'm damned if I'll do it without my pink coat."

The Colonel's son, Godfrey, was away in boarding school and his parents were startled to receive a letter from him which contained the sentence: "Last night I had my first naughty."

His mother was most upset and wrote back to him immediately telling him that under no circumstances was he to have another one.

In time the reply came back, "Don't worry, Mother, I won't. The first one hurt too much."

One morning as they were dressing, the Colonel's wife said to him, "You know, I had a funny dream last night. I dreamed I was at an auction. They were auctioning pricks. The long ones were fetching £300 and the thick ones £450.

"What about the ones like mine?"

"Oh, those," she laughed, "they were giving those away as samples."

The Colonel absorbed this in silence for a moment and then said, "It's funny you should mention that, my dear. I, too, dreamed I was at an auction last night. They were auctioning cunts. The pretty ones were getting £600 and the tight ones £800."

"What about the ones like mine?"

"Oh. That's where they held the auction."

The Colonel's wife woke early one morning while it was still dark. To her surprise the Colonel was getting dressed.

"What time is it?" she asked.

"A quarter to five."

"Where are you going?"

"I couldn't sleep, so I thought I'd go outside and rake some leaves."

The next morning the same thing happened, this time at half past four. When it was repeated at twenty to five on the third morning, she became suspicious. Was it possible that the Colonel might be visiting Mary, the maid, in the early morning?

She devised a plan. Taking Mary aside she said to her, "Mary, your people live up north, don't they?"

"Yes, Madam."

"And since you only have one day off a week, it must be quite a while since you have had a chance to see your mother, I suppose?"

"Yes, Madam."

"Now, Mary, here's what we might do. You prepare the dinner on Friday evening and go off and catch the train north, leaving me to serve the Colonel and clean up afterwards. We can manage without you on Saturday and Sunday, and you can catch the train back on Sunday afternoon. How does that sound?"

"Thank you very much, Madam."

"Just one thing, though. There will be no need to say anything about this to the Colonel. He doesn't like to be bothered about household arrangements. We will just keep it to ourselves."

And so it came about. Mary prepared Friday's dinner and caught the train north. The Colonel ate his meal completely unaware of any change in routine. In due course they retired for the night.

At four-thirty she woke up. The Colonel was dressing.

"What time is it?"

"Half past four."

"Where are you going?"

"I couldn't sleep. I thought I'd go out and rake some leaves."

He left, closing the front door behind him.

She jumped out of bed, and without pausing to put on a gown, slipped down the passage to the maid's bedroom where she climbed into the maid's bed beneath the open window.

About ten minutes had passed when she saw in the half light a shadowy figure climbing in through the window, and into bed with her. Not wishing to spoil the surprise, she did not say a word until the deed was done.

"And now," she said, "I suppose you'll go and rake some more leaves?"

"Rake leaves be damned," was the reply, "I've got four hundred more bottles of milk to deliver."

The Colonel was playing a round of golf with a solicitor friend. On the fourth hole they were held up by two women in the distance who were having some difficulty with their approach shots. The solicitor volunteered to go and speak to the women, and ask if he and Castarse might play through.

He had only walked half-way down the fairway when he turned and hurriedly returned to the Colonel.

"I say, Colonel," he said, "I can't speak to them. That's my wife, and she's playing with my mistress. You go."

The Colonel walked towards the women but soon he, too, turned in his tracks and hurried back.

"I say, old boy. What a coincidence. That's my wife playing with my mistress too. Let's have a cigar while we wait."

A visitor to the Colonel's country club finished a round of golf and headed for the locker room for a shower. Being unfamiliar with the arrangements he mistakenly went into the ladies' locker room, which was deserted, and entered one of the cubicles. By the time he had had his shower and was towelling himself dry, a number of women had entered the locker room and he could hear their voices across the partition.

Having only his towel with which to cover himself, and of course not wishing to be identified, he wrapped the towel round his head and ran naked through the locker room.

Amid the screams he heard the following exchange:

"I don't know who he is, but he's certainly not my husband."
"No, and he's not my husband either."
"Not only that, he's not even a member of this club."

The secretary of the Country Club was disturbed to see from the clubhouse window that a fight was taking place on the ninth green. There were four men involved. One was lying on his back while the other three exchanged punches.

The secretary dashed out to stop the fight.

"What on earth's going on? What are you fighting about? I'll have you all excluded."

The fight stopped. The Colonel pointed to the man on the ground and said, "That's my partner. He's just had a stroke — and these ghouls are trying to add it to our score."

The Reverend Pillsbury was terribly precise and proper. One afternoon he went to the country club for a round of golf. The steward looked for a partner for him and found our redoubtable warrior in the locker room. Without saying anything to the Colonel, he went back to the Rector.

"Sorry, Reverend," he said, "but you don't have much choice today. The only player in the club at present is Colonel Castarse."

"Well, that should be alraight. The Colonel is quaite a faine player Ai'm tewld. Ai should learn a lot from playing with him."

"Oh, you will, you will. It's just that the Colonel does have a tendency — ah — to put it bluntly, he uses an awful lot of strong language in his game. I hate to . . ."

"That's perfectly alraight. Dewn't trouble yourself any further. Please ask Colonel Castarse if he would maind playing with a duffer laike me."

The steward returned to the locker room and asked the Colonel whether he would care to play a round with the Rector.

"Certainly, old chap. Don't care who I thrash."

The game commenced, and was such a success that the players went on for another nine holes.

When they finally returned to the clubhouse, the steward had the opportunity to take the Rector aside and ask him, "Did you run into any difficulty with the Colonel swearing at all?"

"Ew, new. The Colonel was quaite proper in his speech at all taimes. There was ewnly one occasion on which he called upon the Almighty to commit an indecency upon the caddie — not that he didn't thoroughly deserve it, mark you."

The Colonel and Ponsonby had had a lot to drink. The Colonel suddenly asked him, "Ponsonby. Do you like big arses on women?"

"No, of course not."

"And do you like droopy tits?"

"No, I don't."

"How about big, sloppy cunts? Do you like those?"

"No. Look here. What is all this?"

"Well if you don't like big arses and droopy tits and big sloppy cunts, why are you sneaking round after my wife all the time?"

The Colonel's son was horrified to see his father coming out of a notorious brothel.

"Father!" he said, shocked.

"Son," said the Colonel, "say nothing. I prefer the simulated enthusiasm of a paid prostitute to the dignified acquiescence of your mother."

One day the Colonel's wife decided to try and win back her husband's love. On the advice of a woman friend she brought him his slippers and a cigar when he came home late, poured him a cold drink and cuddled up in his lap dressed only in a silk dressing-gown. After a time she murmured, "Let's go upstairs, darling."

"I might as well, " said her bemused husband, "I'll catch hell when I get home anyway."

When their son finished school, his mother insisted that he must go to University, over the protests of the Colonel, who felt that this would be a needless extravagance.

Once established in college, the boy sent home for blazers, creams, rowing togs, tennis togs, and no matter what the Colonel said, Godfrey was refused nothing. Finally he wrote that the college ball was coming soon, and could he have a suit of tails.

The Colonel was outraged, but his wife sent the money.

Afterwards Godfrey wrote that he had been a great success at the ball. "Everyone said I looked like a proper Count."

The Colonel was disgusted. "All that education, and he still can't spell."

During a period when the domestic situation was particularly trying, the Colonel was consoling himself with some rather heavy drinking. He was joined by his friend Carruthers.

"I say, Colonel, you're punishing it a bit there, aren't you? What's it all about? What's on your mind?"

"Oh, it's the wife. She's just let herself go completely, I'm afraid. The home is always a mess — ashtrays overflowing — dirty dishes in the sink — beds unmade. Doesn't look after herself like she used to either — slops around in a dressing gown all day — hair in curlers — yesterday's make-up. I've grown to hate her so much I'd like to do away with her, if only I knew a way of getting away with it."

"You really mean that?"

"My word I do."

"Well, there is a way, you know. Perfectly legal too, if you're prepared to go through with it. Why don't you fuck her to death?"

"What do you mean?"

"Well, women, you know, can only take so much sex, it seems, and then they expire. All you've got to do is go on giving it to her until she conks out, and they can't touch you. You're her husband, after all."

"Jove! I never knew about this. I just might try it."

The next evening, having fortified himself with stout and oysters, the Colonel returned home to find his wife in her usual slovenly condition, and the house a pigsty. Brushing aside the mention of dinner, he swept her into the bedroom, tossed her on the bed and unceremoniously knocked her off.

Later, when she was relaxing and about to go to sleep, he shook her awake and started all over again. Throughout the night he kept repeating the performance, giving her no rest. In the grey light of early morning, he looked hard at her. Her brow was beaded with cold sweat. Her features had taken on a green-grey cast, and she seemed to have stopped breathing.

"I've done it," he told himself. "The perfect crime. Now to dash off to the office, and when I come home this evening I can make the tragic discovery."

He showered, shaved and dressed and headed for the city.

In the evening, having rehearsed his surprise and grief, he was taken aback when he turned the corner to see the lights on in his house. Never mind, he thought, the neighbours must have found the body. His task would be so much easier.

However, as he climbed the stairs of the front porch, who should open the door, but his wife. She was beautifully groomed, made up, permed and perfumed. She wore her best full-length gown, which made her look almost attractive.

Nonplussed, the Colonel looked past her into the house. It was immaculate. And in the dining area he could see the best silver sparkling on the best table linen by the soft flickering light of candles. The savoury aroma of dinner floated in the air. He was dumbfounded.

His wife nudged him. "You look after me, boy, and I'll look after you."

One of the Colonel's tenants had a rather plain daughter, and one day she told her father that she was pregnant. He loaded his shotgun and declared, "He'll marry you — or else . . ."

"He's married already," said the girl. "It was the Colonel."

Her father said he'd shoot him just the same, and headed for The Hall in a rage.

"Here. Hold on a minute, Hodge, old chap," said the Colonel. "I'll do the right thing by the girl. If she has a boy I'll settle a thousand pounds on him. If it should be a girl, five hundred pounds."

"What if it's twins, then?"

"Fifteen hundred. Now be off, you old blackmailer."

"Hang on. One other thing. If it's a miscarriage, can she have another go?"

The Colonel was planning a trip to Madagascar and consulted his physician about vaccinations. The doctor was able to give him all that he needed except one.

"What's that?" asked the Colonel.

"Well," said the medico, "it's a somewhat rare tropical disease called boh-bong."

"Never heard of it. What's it like?"

"It's characterised by extreme lassitude and an exaggerated dropping of the scrotum. However, you'll be able to get fixed up at Cape Town, and, as I say, it's very rare. You're most unlikely to run across a case of it, except in the most remote regions."

Unfortunately the Colonel was so rushed in Cape Town that he entirely forgot the extra vaccination. He did not remember it until he had made the journey to Madagascar, and had been on safari for several weeks. The guide led the party into a typical native kraal — a central clearing surrounded by grass huts built on poles. While the bearers were unloading the luggage, the Colonel was absorbing his surroundings. He saw a man standing in the middle of the clearing, moaning piteously in a loud voice.

"What's the matter with that poor fellow?" he asked the guide.

"Oh. He's got a rather rare disease — boh-bong."

The Colonel shuffled uneasily, remembering that he should have had the necessary shots.

"What's he moaning like that for, then?"

"Well, actually, he's standing on his balls, and he's too tired to lift his feet."

The journey continued without any of the party contracting this dreaded malady. They visited a number of similar villages in the region and gathered much useful information.

At one stop the Colonel was intrigued by two people who appeared to be joined together.

"I say," he asked the guide, "are they Siamese twins?"

"No," was the reply, "just honeymooners."

While he was in Africa, the Colonel undertook to teach one of the natives English. He would point to various objects as they walked through the forest and pronounce the English names for them, whereupon the man would copy him.

"Tree. Tree."

"Tree. Tree."

"Stream. Stream."

"Stream. Stream."

"Rocks. Rocks."

"Rocks. Rocks."

Suddenly they came upon a native man and woman in the act of having sexual intercourse.

"What's that?"

"Ah — bike. Bike."

The native immediately drove his spear into the man's buttock.

"What did you do that for?" asked the Colonel.

"My bike. My bike."

Working amongst the natives in Africa and Madagascar, the Colonel was often able to help them by rendering first aid and administering simple medication. One of the native boys left the compound with a bottle of suppositories, and, as the Colonel thought, explicit instructions for their use.

A few days later, the Colonel met the native and asked him if he was feeling better. The native replied, "No, I am not. For all the good them pills done me I might as well have shoved them up my arse."

The Colonel and his party were pushing through jungle where no white man had ever been before. At last they broke through to the bank of a river where some native girls were bathing together with a naked black man, who had the largest penis ever seen. It was unique, and they asked through the interpreter if they could photograph it for scientific publications.

There was some mumbling and the interpreter returned.

"He wants to know what all the fuss is about. Does not the member of the white man shrink in cold water?"

The Colonel visited an African tribe and was told by its Oxford-educated chief that they did everything just as in jolly old England. He invited the Colonel to attend a court trial, at which he was presiding, where all the lawyers were wearing tasselled wigs, gowns and other appointments, just as in England.

The Colonel was puzzled, however, by a black boy in white gloves who ran through the audience from time to time feeling the women's breasts, without anyone taking any notice of him. He asked why the boy was not put out for disturbing the trial.

"Why, we're doing it the way it's done in England, old chap," the Chief told him. "He's the Court Titter. You know, you're always reading in the accounts of trials, 'A titter ran through the crowd'."

The Colonel was enjoying a lion hunt in Africa. He wounded a pregnant lioness in the bush and then retired gracefully behind his native bush-beaters, saying masterfully, "All right, boys, go in there and get that lioness."

They did not move, but muttered, "Katumbah — Katumbah, bwana."

"You heard me. What are you, a bunch of cowards? Go in there and drag that lioness out."

"Katumbah — Katumbah, bwana."

"What is this nonsense?" the Colonel enquired angrily of the interpreter. "What does 'Katumbah — Katumbah' mean? Are they afraid? Tell them I'll pay double."

"Bwana," said the trembling interpreter. "That just means in our native talk, 'Fuck you, boss. Go in there and get that wounded lioness yourself'."

It was in Africa that the Colonel was invited to participate in a game of African roulette.

"African roulette? I've heard of Russian roulette, of course, but what's this African roulette?"

They explained. "You go into that hut where there are six holes cut in the wall. Behind each hole is an African woman. You choose your hole and poke your prick through. The African woman sucks you off."

"But where does the roulette come in?"

"Oh, one of the African women is a cannibal."

In the 'thirties Colonel Castarse led an extremely formidable expedition from Daru to Kikori across New Guinea's treacherous Ramu Valley. In addition to the considerable hazards of the rugged terrain and dense jungle, the native tribesmen were headhunters, and the swamps and waterways they had to cross were infested with crocodiles.

The original party of thirty-five dwindled at an alarming rate. Fourteen days out of Daru, there remained only the Colonel and his aide. They had been without food for four days, and there had been no fresh water since the previous morning. They dragged themselves through the tropical heat until at last the older man collapsed and could go no further.

"Sergeant," he gasped. "Find some water. I'm all in."

The faithful aide staggered obediently into the dense bush. After more than an hour, he reeled back from the scrub to the prostrate Colonel, who by now was nearly delirious with the heat. He was empty-handed.

"Water! Sergeant! Did you bring water?"

"No, sir. I couldn't."

"You couldn't? In God's name, why not?"

"The river, sir; it's infested with crocodiles."

"Don't take any notice of them. Just bring the water. Those crocodiles are just as frightened of you as you are of them."

"Colonel, if those crocodiles are just as frightened of me as I am of them, then that damned water isn't fit to drink."

Late one afternoon back in London the Colonel went into an American-style drug store.

"Let me have a condom will you? Large size."

Unwrapping the sachet, the Colonel unrolled his purchase and held it over the counter.

"Now would you put three large scoops of chocolate ice cream inside?"

The chemist did so and collected the Colonel's money. Then, unable to contain his curiosity, he asked the Colonel what he was going to do with it.

"Ah, yes. Well, you see, it's my wife's birthday, and over the years I've given her a refrigerator, a washing machine, hot water service, vacuum cleaner, mixer, dishwasher, clothes dryer, television — just about everything you can think of."

"So?"

"So tonight I'm going to give her a deep freeze."

Fairly early in an evening of cards, one of the players rose to his feet.

"I hate to break up the game just when it's getting interesting, but if I don't get home before eleven, my wife will really give me curry."

"Oh, come on," said the Colonel. "You're not properly organised."

"Not organised? I'll tell you how organised I am. Whenever we're going to have a little game, I oil the lock on the back door, and always leave the garage doors and the front gates open when I drive out.

"Now, I live on the side of a hill, and when I go home, I drive round the block, roll down the street with the engine off, along the drive, and into the garage. I take my shoes off outside the back door, let myself in without a sound, and tiptoe down to the bedroom.

"As soon as I get inside the bedroom door, my wife always says, 'And where have you been until this ridiculous hour?'"

"That's just what I said," retorted the Colonel. "You're not properly organised.

"Now I live on the side of a hill, too, but I never go through any of this nonsense of oiling locks, or leaving doors and gates open.

"I drive up the street from the bottom of the hill, in first gear. And when I park the car in the garage I slam the garage doors and slam the front gates.

"I go in the front door, making as much noise as I like, turn on the bedroom light, grab my wife by the arm and say, 'Wake up, love, what about a bit of nonsense?' And you've never seen a woman sleep so soundly."

When the Colonel returned from a camouflaged weekend with his latest lady friend, his wife asked, "How was the fishing trip?"

"Jolly good," the Colonel replied. "We caught quite a few but gave them to the guides. By the way, dear, you forgot to pack the flask of brandy and my shaving lotion."

"I put them in your tackle box," his wife replied stonily.

The Colonel, at the theatre with his wife, went out to the toilet at interval. He went through a wrong door and found himself in a garden. It was too well kept to think of using the ground, so he lifted a plant out of a flower pot and used that, replacing the plant afterwards.

Returning to his seat he found that the next act had already begun and asked his wife in a whisper, "What's happened so far in this act?"

"You ought to know," she replied coldly. "You were in it."

The receptionist at the Carlton checked in a grumpy middle-aged guest.

"What name, please?"

"Castarse. Colonel Castarse." She handed him his key, saying, "Your room is on the fourth floor, Colonel. The bell-boy will bring up your luggage."

As soon as he had finished unpacking, the Colonel picked up the house phone.

"Reception. May I help you?"

"Get me room service."

"What would you like, sir?"

"Send me up a woman. About five foot two. Reasonably good looking. Blonde for preference, but it's not important."

"I'm sorry, sir. This is not that kind of hotel. We are quite unable to provide a service of that sort."

"Balderdash! I'm paying seventeen pounds a day for bed and breakfast, and I expect every convenience. If you can't have someone up here within half an hour, I'm checking out," he said and slammed down the receiver.

After a time there came a discreet knock at the door. The Colonel opened the door and found quite an attractive blonde standing outside.

"All right," he said, "come in."

He closed the door, "Take off your clothes."

The young woman complied.

"Now get into bed."

She did so, and the Colonel himself undressed. Climbing wearily into bed beside her, he said, "Very well. Cross your legs and start nagging. I'm homesick."

The Colonel came home from the lodge dinner and told his wife, "The funniest thing happened. The lodge President said he'd give a new hat to any man who'd get up and say he'd been faithful to his wife since the day they were married. And not a single man got up."

"Very funny. Where's your new hat?"

In the butcher shop, the Colonel's wife was examining an old chicken very suspiciously. She prodded it, poked at its breast, and finally spread its legs wide apart and sniffed its rump very carefully. Then, turning to the butcher, she said elaborately, "Do you have any liver today?"

The butcher was furious. "Look here," he said. "I'll bet you couldn't pass that test either, and you're alive."

The Colonel called James into his study one night and showed him an enormous erection.

"What do you think of that, James?"

"Isn't it a beauty, sir? Shall I call your wife?"

"No, James. Bring me my overcoat and we'll see if we can smuggle this one down to the village."

The Colonel and his wife celebrated their silver wedding anniversary by going on a second honeymoon. They went back to the same town where they had spent their honeymoon twenty-five years before, stayed at the same hotel, and even had the same suite of rooms.

They unpacked their luggage and went down to the dining room for dinner and a bottle of wine. At a quarter to nine they returned to their suite and began to prepare for bed.

The Colonel's wife said, "Reginald, you remember the first time we came here twenty-five years ago. You went into that room there and I went into this room here. We both got undressed and when I was ready, I called out to you, and we ran into each other's arms, and we stayed that way all night. You do remember, don't you?"

"Yes, I remember."

"Wasn't it romantic?"

"I suppose so."

"Well, why don't we do it again?"

"All right."

The Colonel sighed and went into the dressing room. He got undressed and stood shivering and covered with goose-pimples until he heard, "Yoo-hoo! Reginald! I'm ready."

They both charged out, but this time they missed. The Colonel ran through a full-length opened window and plunged two storeys into a garden bed. When he came to his senses, he was lying in the dirt, without a stitch of clothing, and an attendant from the hotel was standing nearby on the pathway, looking at him.

"Is there something I can do for you, sir?"

"Yes. For God's sake get me a blanket so I can get back up to my room."

"That won't be necessary, sir. You can go as you are."

"Oh, I say. What about all the guests in the lobby?"

"There are no guests in the lobby, sir."

"There must be. It's only nine o'clock,"

"Oh no, sir. They're all up on the second floor, watching some old fowl trying to get her cunt off a doorknob."

The Colonel's wife consulted the doctor. She was perturbed by her pubic hair turning powdery red. The doctor was puzzled.

"How often do you have intercourse with your husband?"

"Oh, just like everybody else."

"Well, how often? Twice a week?"

"Oh, no."

"Twice a month?"

"No."

"Twice a year?"

"Sometimes —"

"I see," said the doctor. "There's nothing to worry about. It's rust."

The Colonel's wife asked him, quite unexpectedly, "If I died, Reginald, would you remarry?"

"That's a morbid question to spring on me, my dear, but, to be frank, in due time I probably would."

"Would you bring your second wife to live here?"

"Since the house is all paid for, yes."

"Would you let her wear my mink coat?"

"It would make more sense than losing money selling it."

"I suppose you'd even let the hussy who replaced me use my custom-crafted golf clubs!" she exploded.

"No, no, my dear. Not that. She happens to be left-handed."

The Colonel's wife was riding round the estates with James. Away on a grassy bank she thought she saw something unusual.

"James," she said. "What do you see over there?"

"A blanket, Madam."

"And what is it doing, James?"

"Moving up and down, Madam."

"Do you see anything else, James?"

"A pair of lady's legs wide apart, Madam."

"What else do you see?"

"A pair of gentleman's legs between them."

"And what do you think they're doing, James?"

"Having intercourse, Madam."

"Good Lord. Does that still go on?"

The Colonel and his wife were spending a day at the zoo. After visiting the bears and the elephants and the big cats they came to the monkeys. The Colonel's wife noticed that the gorilla was sitting close to the bars and seemed to be beckoning.

"Look," she said to the Colonel. "He seems to be trying to attract our attention. Let's go over and see what he wants."

They approached the gorilla's cage, but as soon as they were near enough, the gorilla reached through the bars with a long arm, grabbed the Colonel's wife, and dragged her into the cage, whereupon he began tearing her clothes off. She stood there screaming to the Colonel, "What will I do? What will I do?"

Said the Colonel, "Tell him you've got a headache and you're too tired."

One afternoon the Colonel was enjoying a round of golf with a friend. When they were on the twelfth green, the Colonel was about to putt out when he saw a funeral approaching along the road beside the golf course. He at once removed his cap, reversed his putter and bowed his head. His friend was taken by surprise, but did the same.

When the cars had passed, the Colonel put his cap back on and finished the hole as though nothing had happened. As they were walking towards the thirteenth tee his friend remarked, "I say, Castarse, that was a very thoughtful gesture of yours, stopping the game when that funeral went past. I was very impressed."

"Oh I don't know," replied the Colonel. "It was the least I

could do, really. We would have been married twenty-six years next Tuesday."

After the game they made their way to the bar for a few quiet brandies.

"Look here, Castarse," said his partner. "Did you ever see an ice cube with a hole in it?"

"See one?" he snorted. "I was married to one for twenty-six years."

# REGROUPING

After Sunday dinner, the Colonel took his son into the library. "My boy," he began, "it's time for us to have a little talk. You're twenty years of age. You know the facts of life. You've been to Eton and Cambridge. You've knocked about for a few years. Now it's time you thought about settling down and getting married.

"When I die, all these estates, all my interests in the city will pass on to you, and I would like to know that you in turn had someone to pass them on to.

"Now, take the Lady Muriel. She's a good healthy sort. Plays a good stick of tennis and golf. Not a bad seat on a horse. She'd be a good breeder. Why don't you marry the Lady Muriel?"

"But, Father. I don't love the Lady Muriel."

"Oh, love is it? Well what about the Lady Cynthia? She's a nice little piece of goods. A charming hostess and a pretty dancer. Just the sort of girl to smooth away the worries after a hard day in the city. Why don't you marry the Lady Cynthia?"

"But, Father. I don't love the Lady Cynthia."

"Well damn it all, who do you love?"

"Well, Father, I am rather keen on Lord Lonsdale."

"Lord Lonsdale? You can't marry him. He's a Catholic!"

Ultimately the Colonel's son went through Theological College and took Holy Orders. The Colonel saw him only occasionally.

Smythe was an army PT instructor who finished his time in the Far East. To the disappointment of his family he took a job there, instead of returning to England.

Several times his Dad wrote asking what the job was, but he always evaded the question. At last he came home on a long vacation and his Dad took him out for a few drinks.

"Now, Son," he said, "Out with it. What's this job you're doing?"

"Smythe explained that he had a really well-paid job at the court of one of these wealthy oil sheikhs.

"Yes, but what?"

"Well, Dad, it's a kind of educational job."

"Educational? Why, you bloody dunce, you were always bottom of the class. Come on. You can trust your old Dad, can't you?"

"Well, Dad. It's like this. I've got a wall painted black, and I get sent a lot of well-made fourteen-year-old virgins from the village. My job is to teach them arithmetic."

"Do you mean to say you get a fancy salary just for that?"

"Now hang on a minute, Dad. It isn't that easy. It takes perseverance. But when they pass out fully trained, the Boss is very satisfied."

"But what do they have to do to pass out?"

"When they can hold a stick of chalk in the cheeks of their arse, and write on the wall one and seventeen thirty-seconds plus three and twenty-nine sixty-fourths equals four and sixty-three sixty-fourths, they're ready for the Sultan's harem."

In the officers' club one evening the Colonel and some of his associates were reminiscing about former days when somebody asked, "Whatever became of Featherstonwhore?"

"Oh, didn't you know? He was cashiered in South Africa."

"What on earth for?"

"He was caught having sexual relations with an ostrich."

"Good heavens. Was it a male ostrich or a female ostrich?"

"Oh, a female of course. There was never anything unnatural about Featherstonwhore."

Carruthers was filling the members' glasses from a whisky bottle when he was stopped by the padre, who covered his glass.

"None for me, thank you. I'd sooner commit adultery."

Straightaway the Colonel began pouring his drink back into the bottle.

"I never realised we had a choice."

One of the Colonel's good friends at the club was warned off smoking cigars because they were killing him. However, he was unable to break the habit. The chaplain told the Colonel of a way to help his friend give up cigars.

"All you have to do is buy a box of cigars, unwrap them, stick each one up your rear end and roll it around a little. Then carefully rewrap each one and give them to him. I assure you he will not smoke many more cigars."

The Colonel followed his advice. Soon after, his friend stopped smoking and remarked, "I've decided to stop smoking cigars. They've started to taste shitty."

But now the Colonel had a new problem for the chaplain, "How do I overcome this awful urge I have to stick cigars up my arse?"

The Colonel came home from his club one night to find James, his butler, sitting in his favourite armchair, smoking one of his cigars, drinking a glass of his brandy, and reading one of his books.

Without rising, James said to the Colonel, "Excuse me, sir. A short time ago I came across a foreign expression with which I am not familiar. Perhaps you could explain to me the meaning of *faux pas*."

The Colonel replied, "*Faux pas*. It's a French expression. I could explain it simply by telling you it's a social blunder, but perhaps if I gave you an illustration it would make it more clear.

"The other week when we were having the garden party in

the country, you will recall Sir Winston Churchill taking Lady Astor for a walk through the rose garden. While they were there Sir Winston got a thorn in his thumb.

"When they came back inside, Lady Astor said to Sir Winston, 'How's your prick, Winston?' and he said, 'Still throbbing, thanks', and I said 'Shit!' and you dropped the soup. That, James, was a *faux pas.*"

The Colonel was giving a dinner party and, of course, James was supervising the arrangements.

Everything was going smoothly when James saw to his horror that as one of the ladies, who was wearing an extremely low-cut gown, leaned forward over the table, one of her breasts fell out.

As quick as a flash James grabbed a soup ladle and did the necessary. It all happened so quickly that none of the guests was aware that anything unusual had happened. The lady rewarded James with a gracious smile of thanks.

When the guests had departed, the Colonel complimented James on the success of his arrangements and added, "By the

way, James. That little incident that took place with the Lady Millicent. Very quick thinking, James, but next time — a warm spoon, eh, James?"

The Colonel was delighted to be taking to dinner a young woman who was both beautiful and voluptuous. But he was dismayed when the waiter took their order, for she proceeded to order all the most expensive dishes.

Somewhat staggered, he asked, "Do you always eat like this at home?"

"No," she replied. "But then, no one there wants to sleep with me."

The Salvation Army band played loudly and enthusiastically near the busy intersection as the young workers made their way among the crowd shaking their tambourines and wooden collection boxes. A new recruit approached the Colonel.

"Won't you please give something for penitent fallen women?"

"Sorry, old thing," he replied, "but I'm already giving direct."

One of the companies of which the Colonel was a director asked him to go to the United States to conclude an important business transaction. While he was there he became fascinated by the American practice of telling funny stories, even though he didn't understand any of them. He determined to learn a typical American joke that he could tell the other members of the board on his return.

At last the occasion presented itself. An American business-man asked him, "Suppose you got this crossroad, you see? And coming towards it on another road is a guy on foot. And coming towards it on another road is a guy on a push-bike. And coming towards it on another road is a guy on horse-back. And coming along the last road is a beautiful blonde. Now, which of the three men knew the blonde?"

The Colonel was completely at a loss. "I'm sure I haven't the faintest idea," he said.

"The horse manure. Get it?" the American said. "The horseman knew her."

The Colonel laughed politely, but still wasn't too sure. On his return to London he reported to the board the satisfactory completion of the business and then told the members:

"While I was over there I heard a humorous story that struck me as typical of the American sense of humour. It seems that there is an intersection of two roads. Coming towards the junction one way is a pedestrian, another way is a cyclist, another way is an equestrian and another way an attractive girl. Now the question is, which of the three men knew the girl? And the answer is horse shit, but I don't know how they get it."

Visiting the military hospital, the Colonel was amazed to find Featherstonwhore in one of the wards. He was in a shocking state, obviously very weak, and a mass of bandages.

"Good Lord! Featherstonwhore! Whatever happened to you?"

"Hallo, Castarse, old chap. It's a long story really. After that business in South Africa, I was a bit at a loose end.

"I was invited to go on a safari with the Lady Muriel. We spent simply weeks trekking into the interior with dozens of bearers. Then, dash it all, we were captured by a tribe of natives who practised buggery.

"Well, you know, I went to school at Cheam and it wasn't so bad for me, but the Lady Muriel was furious.

"When we finally got out of that situation, I got in tow with some other ex-service types who were rather musical, and we formed a little band, you know.

"We got a job in a sort of circus and medicine show, and travelled all up the East Coast, through Egypt and the Middle East.

"One of the sultans we played for liked our music so much that he ordered that all our instruments be filled with gold pieces."

"I say. That was a good show."

"Well yes, but actually at the time I was playing the

piccolo. Some of the other fellows did rather well out of it, though.

"So I took up the bass tuba, you know — the big fellow that wraps around the waist and comes out over your shoulder. An enormous thing, really."

"And did you have it filled with gold pieces?"

"Well, actually, no — dash it all. The next johnnie we played for didn't take to our style of music at all. He hated it. In fact, he hated it so much that he ordered that all our instruments be shoved up our arses. That's why I'm here. Lucky to be alive, I expect."

Feeling like a round of golf to relax during the week, the Colonel headed for the country club. There was no one else about so he decided to play alone.

His drive from the first tee was strong, but sliced away through a screen of trees separating the fairway from the roadway. Considering the situation for a few moments, the Colonel decided to take a two-stroke penalty, and a new ball.

His second drive was long and strong and straight in the direction of the pin. He was quite elated but took his time wheeling his trolley down the fairway and making ready his approach shot.

He had selected his club and was addressing the ball when behind him on the fairway there began a loud commotion. Turning, he saw the club secretary making his way down from the clubhouse waving and shouting.

As he came closer, the Colonel asked him. "What's all the fuss about, old boy?"

"I say, Colonel. Do you know what you've done?"

"Well, yes. I sliced my first drive through the trees there by the road and took a new ball — with a two-stroke penalty, of course."

"Yes, but Colonel. You don't realise what you've done. That first ball of yours went through the trees on to the road. It hit a young girl in the eye and she fell off her push-bike. A young chap behind her on a motorbike swerved to avoid her and went into a ditch. His front wheel is buckled out of shape, and he's got a broken arm. Coming the other way was a bus full of women bowlers. They ran into a tree and a number of women have minor injuries."

"Good Lord! What shall I do? Whatever shall I do?"

"Well if I were you, old boy, I'd be inclined to bring that right thumb over ever so slightly."

The Colonel and Carruthers were playing a round of golf together and Carruthers was impressed by how much the Colonel's game had improved.

"I say, Castarse. You've certainly lifted your game since the last time we played. Have you been getting some coaching from the pro?"

"No, no. It's not that. It's these new bifocals I got from the eye doctor. They're a tremendous help when you're playing.

"You see, I look down and I can see two balls, a big one and a little one. And when I look at the green I can see two holes, a big one and a little one. All I do then is hit the little ball into the big hole. Very simple really."

"Sounds wonderful. I'll get a pair from the eye doctor myself. It's time I had a new prescription."

Carruthers had the spectacles made and the first time he wore them to the country club, he played a round with the Colonel again. Everything was working like a charm. He kept hitting the little ball into the big hole and both their scores were low.

At the end of the first nine holes, Carruthers went into the locker room to relieve himself. When he came out he was a mess. All the front of his trousers was sopping wet.

"What on earth happened to you?" the Colonel asked him.

Carruthers was shamefaced. "Well, when I went into the toilet, I undid my fly and took my prick out. I had a look and there were two pricks, one small one and one great big one. Well, I knew that wasn't mine, so I put it back in again."

A parson visiting the country club for a game of golf was invited by a stranger to play a round.

"I hope you don't mind, Reverend, but we always play for a pound in this club."

The parson did not approve of gambling, and was rather

put out. Still, he thought, 'only a pound', and teed off. His opponent played dirty, sneezed at the wrong time, used filthy language, cheated whenever he could, and finished up thrashing the poor old parson.

"In this club, the loser buys the drinks. And may I trouble you for six pounds?"

"I thought we agreed on a pound."

"Of course. A pound a hole."

Over drinks, the blighter said, "If you're ever down this way again, Vicar, do drop in. I'll always be glad to give you a game."

"Yes," replied the parson. "Here's my card. You should come to my church. It would be a good idea if you brought your parents, too."

"Brought my mother and father? Why?"

"So that I could marry them for you."

The Colonel was playing a round of golf with Carruthers. At the fourth hole, Carruthers complained of feeling ill.

"Colonel," he said, "I don't feel well at all. Let's go back to the clubhouse."

"Buck up, old chap. See if you can play a few more holes. The fresh air will do you good."

But at the fifth hole, Carruthers complained again, "Colonel, I can't go on. My stomach's not right at all."

The Colonel tried to cheer him up.

"Just take a few deep breaths and you'll be all right."

"But look here, I don't feel at all well. The fact is that at the fourth hole, I let a fart."

"Not to worry, old boy. That can happen to any of us."

"Yes, but Colonel," wailed Carruthers, "the trouble is — I followed through."

While staying in a country hotel, the Colonel rang down to the reception desk and said, "Send up a nice whore."

The proprietor's wife was very angry and told her husband to go up and throw the man out. He refused, saying the request was natural and harmless, and that he didn't want to lose a good customer.

54

"Well, if you won't throw him out, I will," she said, and marched upstairs.

There was a fearful uproar for about twenty minutes, after which the Colonel came down and said to the proprietor, "I suppose that's the best you can get in country towns, but she was a tough old bitch. I damned near had to rape her."

The Colonel was in the habit of lunching regularly with three other prominent men in the town. There was the local bank manager, the superintendent of the Sunday school and the proprietor of the general store. One day, the conversation turned to secret vices. They all agreed that everyone had a secret vice.

The bank manager admitted, "I've got a secret vice. Everyone has. Mine's horse racing. Of course, it wouldn't do for it to get around, or people would lose confidence in the bank. But it's all quite harmless, really. I take my holidays during the spring carnival and off I go. I bet really big, too, but never with the bank's money. Whether I win or lose I always have a marvellous time, and when I come back I settle down and wait until next time."

The Sunday school superintendent was the next to speak. "Of course everyone has a secret vice," he said. "Although it wouldn't do for anyone else to know, I don't mind telling you that mine's drink. Every so often I get the urge and I go off on a 'business trip' and drink myself stupid for days on end. When it's over I feel better, and come back to leading a normal life. Of course, I keep it a secret because you know how my church is about drinking."

The Colonel was next. "Well, I must admit that I have my secret vice too. I keep it quiet, but I know it'll be all right to tell you chaps. It's a little widow. It's all very discreet. She lives about sixty miles away and was rather lonely. I see that she's kept comfortable, and there you are. Everyone's happy."

"The three then turned on the fourth man. "Come on, old chap. Tell us your secret vice. You must have one."

"Oh, I've got one all right, but it's too awful to tell you fellows."

"Of course it's not. We've told you ours. Now you must tell us yours."

They pestered him until finally he gave in. "Well, if you must know, it's gossip, and I can hardly wait to get out of this room."

The local Society for the Investigation of Psychic Phenomena was meeting in the village hall to hear an address by a famous spiritualist.

When she had finished her lecture she said to the audience, "Now I'm sure someone in our little gathering tonight must have had the fascinating experience of having had sexual intercourse with a ghost. Would you care to share your experiences with the rest of us? We'd all be most interested. Now don't be shy."

From the back of the hall, a voice said, "Well, actually, I have."

It was Featherstonwhore. As he came forward there was a polite round of applause.

The chairman announced, "We will now have the pleasure of hearing from Mr Featherstonwhore, who will tell us about his experience of having sexual intercourse with a ghost."

Featherstonwhore shuffled awkwardly. "I say. This is most embarrassing. I thought you said 'goat'."

Featherstonwhore was travelling in a locked compartment on a train without a toilet. He asked the only other occupant, an American, for permission to relieve himself on a spread newspaper, which he subsequently folded up and flung out of the window.

Unable to avoid watching the entire procedure, the American lit up a long black cigar to cover some of the odour.

"I say," said Featherstonwhore, "you know this is a non-smoking compartment."

At a dinner party one night, the Colonel's companion was a very charming American lady. During the course of the dinner he asked her, "I say, my dear. Would you possibly consider sleeping with me for one night for, say, five thousand pounds?"

She smiled charmingly, "You just name the time, Colonel."

"Well then," he went on, "is it possible that you might consider sleeping with me for five pounds?"

"Say, Colonel, what kind of a girl do you take me for?"

"Oh, we've already established that, my dear. Now we're haggling about the price."

One evening in a cocktail bar the Colonel met an attractive girl who took him home to her flat, cooked him a beautiful meal and served it by candlelight. After dinner she took him to bed with her and made passionate love to him.

In the morning while he was showering and dressing she prepared him a sumptuous breakfast. As he was leaving she said to him, "Wait a minute. What about the money?"

To which the Colonel replied, "Oh no, my dear, an officer of the British Army would never dream of accepting money."

Dining alone in a first-class restaurant, the Colonel called the wine waiter over and said, "Bring me a bottle of 1944 dry red from the eastern slopes."

When the wine waiter brought the bottle and opened it, the Colonel tasted the contents.

"No, no," he said, "this is 1942 from the southern slopes."

The waiter examined the label and admitted that the Colonel was right. A fresh bottle was brought. Again the Colonel tasted. "No, no," he said, "this is 1945 from the northern slopes."

Once more the waiter examined the label and found that the Colonel was perfectly correct. Again he brought a fresh bottle. The Colonel took one sip.

"No, no," he said, "this is 1943 from the western slopes!"

The waiter went away again.

A drunk in the corner had been watching all this, fascinated. He approached the Colonel with a glass in his hand.

"Would you mind tasting this?"

"Certainly," said the Colonel. He took a swig and sputtered. "That's piss," he exclaimed.

"Yes I know," said the drunk, "but how old am I?"

The Colonel often dined in first-class restaurants and he had a fine appreciation of good cuisine. But on one such evening he had a very unsettling experience. He saw the doddering old waiter shuffle to his table with his thumb deep in the consommé. He held his peace.

Later he watched the old man bring his lasagna, and again his thumb was deep in the sauce. He still said nothing. After all, the restaurant was one of London's finest.

For dessert he had coupé marron, but this time the waiter did not put his thumb in the ice cream. The Colonel could contain himself no longer.

"See here, my man," he addressed the waiter. "Why is it you put your finger in the soup and the sauce, but not in the ice cream?"

The waiter was unperturbed. "It's simple really," he said. "I suffer badly from arthritis and warm things relieve the pain in my thumb."

The Colonel was livid. "You decrepit old toad! Putting your thumb in my food! Why don't you take your thumb and stick it up your arse?"

"The customers wouldn't like it, sir. I can only do that in the kitchen."

On a long and tedious train journey the Colonel was shut up all morning in a "dog box" compartment with only one other passenger, who was a reasonably attractive woman. Wishing to make the best possible use of the time, he struck up a conversation with her.

"I say, the fields look really topping after the rain, what?"
"Yes."
"Look at all those spring lambs gambolling on the hillside. Pretty terrific, what?"
"I suppose so."
"Doesn't the river look really beautiful, winding its way through the hills? Reflections and all that."
"Yes."
"Enough of this love talk! Off with your pants."

After the Colonel's return from a weekend house party, the Admiral met him at the club and said, "I say, Castarse, how was the Duke's weekend house party?"

"Well, actually, if the soup had been as warm as the beer, and the beer had been as cold as the chambermaid, and the

chambermaid had been as hot as the Duchess, it would've been a jolly good show."

Ponsonby was also a weekend guest at the Duke's estate. In the middle of the night, he had to answer an urgent call of nature but couldn't manage to find the bathroom. In his distress, he roamed into the conservatory, found a high jardiniere, clambered up and perched on it to relieve himself. Disturbed about what he had done, he quietly dressed and left the mansion before dawn.

For the next two days, the stench was unbearable.

On the third day, Ponsonby received a telegram from the Duke, "All is forgiven, but where did you hide it?"

The Colonel developed a persistent knocking in his head and a ringing in his ears. Two physicians he consulted told him the same thing. He had six months to live.

Typically, he decided he would go out in a blaze of glory. He would buy a yacht, travel, throw parties, get a new sports car, a new wardrobe. He decided to start on the wardrobe.

He called at his favourite outfitters in Bond Street, and headed for the shirt department.

"I want a dozen shirts," he told the young assistant.

"Do you mind if I measure your collar size, sir?"

"That won't be necessary. I wear size sixteen."

"If you don't mind, sir, we are trained to always measure customers for size. Would you mind, sir?"

"Oh, very well. But I should know what size shirt I wear. I've been wearing size sixteen for the last ten years."

The assistant put the tape around the Colonel's collar.

"Oh, I beg your pardon, sir, but your correct collar size is seventeen."

"That's ridiculous. I've been wearing sixteens for the last ten years."

"If you've worn sixteens for the last ten years, you'd have a knocking in your head and a ringing in your ears."

A few weeks before Christmas, the postmaster came across a letter addressed to:

Santa Claus, North Pole

Opening it, as he always did in such cases, he read this unusually pathetic message:

Dear Santa Claus,

Do you think it might be possible to give me thirty pounds for Christmas?

It is not only for myself that I write, but for my widowed mother and my three little sisters. Thirty pounds would buy me a new bike, and with it I can get a job after school delivering the evening paper. It's worth fifteen shillings a week and my mother could certainly put it to good use, as the only other money she has is the pension.

I know that you have a lot of calls on you, but I hope you can help me too.

Yours sincerely,
Paul Meldrum
4a Ashby Street
MALTBY

The postmaster was so impressed that he took the letter along to the next meeting of the Masonic lodge where the Colonel was the master.

The letter was read out and the brothers, with the Colonel's encouragement, had a really generous "whip around" which raised twenty-six pounds. The postmaster arranged to deliver it to the boy in a Masonic envelope.

A few days after Christmas another letter arrived at Maltby Post Office addressed in the same handwriting:

Santa Claus
North Pole

The Postmaster didn't bother to open the letter of thanks, but took it along to the next lodge meeting where it was read aloud:

Dear Santa Claus,

Thank you very much indeed for sending me the money for my new bike, only next time you do this sort of thing, be sure not to send it through the Masons as the bastards cheated me out of four pounds.

Yours sincerely,
Paul Meldrum

Every Christmas Eve the Colonel would play Santa Claus to

the children in the village. Dressed in traditional costume, and with extra whiskers to complete the illusion, he visited all the homes and left a toy in each waiting stocking.

One such Christmas Eve he was tiptoeing across a bedroom from the fireplace when a lovely young blonde sat up unexpectedly in the bed. She was, he judged, about nineteen years, and very shapely. The diaphanous blue nightie she was wearing did nothing to conceal a ripe figure.

"Hello, Santie," she said.

"Oh! Excuse me, Miss," said the Colonel. "I thought this room belonged to a little boy. He'd be about nine now."

"That's my young cousin. He has the room across the hall now."

"Well, I'll be getting along. I'm sorry to have disturbed you."

"Won't you stay with me a little while, Santie? I'm lonely."

"That's very kind of you, but I'm afraid I can't. I have a lot of calls to make and tonight's my busy night."

The young woman pouted and slipped off one shoulder strap, exposing a very shapely breast.

"Just for a little while, Santie? Please?"

"My dear, I'd love to, really I would. If it was any other night — but I can't disappoint all those little boys and girls."

She slipped off the other shoulder strap and the nightdress fell to her waist.

"Come on, Santie. You can spare a few minutes if you really want to."

Resolutely the Colonel headed for the door. Seeing him about to leave, the young woman threw back the covers and swung both long, shapely legs out of the bed. She stood up. The nightdress fell about her ankles. She stretched out her arms.

"Please, Santie."

In a rage the Colonel threw his sack of toys to the floor.

"Bugger it! I might as well," he exploded. "I'll never get back up the chimney like this anyway."

One moonlit night the Colonel was fishing from a small boat with his two friends, the Presbyterian Minister and the Vicar. Presently the Presbyterian Minister stood up.

"Excuse me, gentlemen. I have to answer a call of nature."

Stepping out of the right side of the boat he walked across the water to the bank twenty feet away. Presently he returned the same way.

After a time the Colonel, too, said that he would answer a call of nature. He stepped out of the right side of the boat, walked across the water to the bank and returned in the same way a few minutes later.

This was too much for the Vicar, who decided that he could not be left out. He stepped out of the left side of the boat and at once sank out of sight.

The Presbyterian Minister chided the Colonel: "I thought you told him about that sandbank."

In a first-class railway compartment, two beautifully dressed ladies were discussing clothes while the Colonel pretended to be asleep in the corner. When one lady said she found the cost of clothes exorbitant, the other suggested she should follow her example and take a boyfriend on the side.

"He'll give you five hundred a month for a little present — your husband would never do that."

"But what if I can't get a friend with five hundred pounds?"

"Then take two with two hundred and fifty each."

The Colonel spoke up, "Listen, ladies, I'm going to sleep now. Wake me up when you get down to twenty pounds."

The guests at the party in Colonel Castarse's London flat were having a wonderful evening. The Colonel was the perfect host as well as the life of the party. The serving of cocktails and the cold buffet had been supervised by James, the butler, and of course everything was all that could be hoped for.

As the *pièce de résistance*, the guests were asked to be seated and the Colonel brought out a midget, dressed in white tie and tails, who sat at the grand piano and rendered such wonderful pieces as the 'Moonlight Sonata', 'Warsaw Concerto', 'Rhapsody in Blue' and many others. The guests were delighted.

As they were leaving, one of the guests took the Colonel aside and asked him, "I say, Castarse. Where did you unearth that marvellous little midget chap?"

The Colonel modestly replied, "Well, actually, it was because I had the chance to do a lady a favour. Afterwards it turned out that she was a witch and had magical powers. She offered to grant me one wish. Any wish.

"Unfortunately she was a little hard of hearing. She thought I asked for a fifteen-inch pianist."

After weeks of waiting and preparation the day of the local fox hunt was at hand. The Colonel dressed for the occasion impeccably, saddled his favourite mare, and rode off to join the other contestants, taking along his champion bitch, unaware of the fact that she was on heat.

Presently came the cry of "Tally Ho", the hounds bayed in pursuit, and there was the familiar stirring ring of the huntsman's horn.

The pack followed the fox through two fields and a hedge and into a wood. The riders emerging from the wood lost sight of the pack and could hear no baying to guide them.

They were in a quiet lane, and leaning over the gate of a small cottage was a yokel, drawing placidly on a clay pipe.

The Colonel addressed him, "I say, old chap, where's the fox?"

The yokel took the pipe from his mouth.

"Well, zorr. When last zeen, 'e worr loying third."

A former hardware merchant who had retired near Maltby badly wanted to join the gentry and sent such large contributions to the hunt club that the Committee felt obliged to let him join.

After the first meet, Colonel Castarse took the new member aside.

"Look here, Bloggs, old boy, do you mind if I give you a word of advice?"

"I ain't bleedin' fussy. Say what yer likes."

"Well, old man, it is customary, when the fox is sighted, to shout 'Tally Ho!', not 'Get cracking, you lousy buggers. There the little bastard goes'."

Living not far from the Colonel was a married couple and the husband became very enthusiastic about the publicity put out by Australia House. He discussed this with his wife.

"'Appen we moight migrate to Orstralia, loov."

"Oo nor. 'Ow about them blackfellows and woild animals? Too dangerous."

"Can't be dangerous, loov. Orstralia 'Ouse be advertoising."

"Well you foind out more about it before you do anything foinal."

"Can't go to Loondon to Orstralia 'Ouse. Too far. 'Appen Oi'll go down to lorcal council and see what they can tell me."

In due course he told his story at the local council, but the official there was not very helpful.

"I'm afraid we don't have any information about migrating to Australia here at all."

"Aye. Aw well. 'Appen Oi'll 'ave to go down to Loondon to Orstralia 'Ouse."

"Oh, there's no need to go to all that trouble. Why don't you go and have a talk to Colonel Castarse? He was seconded to the Woomera rocket range for a time after the war. I'm sure he'll be only too pleased to set you right."

So he told his tale to the Colonel.

"Australia, eh? Haw! Haw! Magnificent country. If I were twenty years younger, I'd migrate there myself. And as for the Australians, they're the most wonderful race of people on earth — warm-hearted, open, generous — they'll even share their wives with you."

"Well in that case, 'appen Oi'll go anyway, even if the old wooman doosn't want to go."

"Half your luck. Wish I were going with you. Just one word of warning, though. Watch out for those white fellows. They hate pommies."

The Colonel and a friend were enjoying a round of golf. His friend was just setting up a putt on the third green when a nude girl rushed out of the nearby trees. Close behind her in hot pursuit came several distinguished-looking men in white coats, one of whom was carrying a bucket of sand.

Unruffled, the golfers continued their game, only to see the same sight on the next two greens. Finally the Colonel caught the attention of one of the men in white and asked him what was happening.

"She's our patient," he explained. "She has this obsession about running nude around a golf course."

"I see," said the Colonel. "But why is your colleague carrying a bucket full of sand?"

"That's his handicap," replied the attendant. "He caught her yesterday."

The Colonel was making an overnight journey in the slowest, most miserable train he had ever seen. He had reserved a sleeping berth, but was not at all encouraged when he inspected it. There was a tiny compartment off the corridor, with few amenities, and the two berths were one above the other.

When the train had moved off, there was no sign of any traveller to occupy the other berth, so, when he was ready to retire, the Colonel settled himself in the upper berth to avoid having someone climb past him during the night.

He slept fitfully. Whenever the train stopped he would be awakened by the lights and shouting on the platform. Only when they moved off would he doze off until the next station.

It was after one such stop, at about midnight, that the Colonel was abruptly awakened by a loud bang as the sliding door of his compartment was flung open. This was followed by two heavy thumps as two suitcases were hurled in.

The Colonel was ready to express his opinion of this lack of consideration when he saw from his vantage point that his travelling companion was a good-looking blonde.

He moved back almost out of sight and, with one eye peering over the edge of the bunk, he watched the young lady first unpack a few things, and then proceed to disrobe.

When she had divested herself of nearly all her garments, and the Colonel was beginning to really enjoy the show, he was rather taken aback to see her remove a blonde wig and toss it on the shelf. She was as bald as an egg.

Next came a full set of false teeth which she soaked in a glass. Then she took out a glass eye which was carefully placed in a velvet-lined box.

By the time she had removed a pair of false breasts, and unhitched an artifical leg, the Colonel was flabbergasted.

At this point she caught sight of him, his eyes bugging over the top bunk.

"What the bloody hell do you want?" she demanded.

"You know what I want, my dear. Unscrew it and hand it up."

The Colonel was weekending at the castle of a member of the peerage. As usual in such castles, the rooms were enormous, the furniture grandiose, but the plumbing facilities pitifully meagre. On Sunday morning he woke up bleary eyed and went in search of the one small bathroom he had been told was somewhere in his wing. He finally stumbled into the room to find the Duchess taking her bath. With a brief "beg pardon" the Colonel beat a hasty retreat.

Fearing that he might be considered less than a gentleman unless he reported the incident, he quietly dressed and went to his host's study, to recount the incident in full to the Duke. His lordship listened without moving a muscle, and then remarked, "Skinny bitch, isn't she?"

The Admiral's daughter upset her parents by announcing her intention of marrying an able seaman. They both approved of her having a naval wedding, but felt that the groom should be at least a petty officer. However, the young woman was quite determined and they resigned themselves to the inevitable. But the Admiral's wife allowed herself one word of caution not long before the wedding.

"If he ever says to you 'Let's do it the other way', promise you won't."

The daughter was duly married and several months went by without her sailor husband saying anything about "doing it the other way". She became quite intrigued, and suggested it to him herself.

"Let's do it the other way," she said.

"What?" he replied. "Fill the house up with a whole lot of screaming kids?"

Being a Justice of the Peace, the Colonel on occasion took his turn on the bench at the local assizes, and some very colourful episodes were acted out there.

On one occasion an Irishman was accused by his neighbour of cracking a jug which he had borrowed.

The Irishman defended himself on three grounds. In the first place, he never had the jug. In the second, it was cracked when he got it. And finally, it was in perfect condition when he returned it.

On another occasion, a man was brought before him charged with indecent exposure. It seemed that he had been apprehended walking down the main street without any trousers. The Colonel was determined to make an example of him, but nevertheless addressed the defendant, "Are you a married man?"

"I am, sir."

"How long have you been married?"

"Four years."

"Do you have any children?"

"Yes. Fourteen."

"Fourteen children? In four years?"

"Well, sir, the first year that we were married my wife presented me with twins."

"Twins. Yes. I see."

"And the second year, she presented me with triplets."

"Triplets, eh? Let's see. That's two and three are five. Go on."

"And the next year she had quadruplets."

"Quadruplets! Two and three are five and four are nine. Yes."

"And this year she gave birth to quintuplets."

"And that makes fourteen. Amazing. Case dismissed."

The sergeant protested.

"But, sir. What about the charge of indecent exposure?"

"Case dismissed. This poor devil hasn't even had time to put his trousers on."

In a preliminary hearing for a divorce suit, the Colonel asked a sailor to describe, in his own words, the events that took place on the afternoon of the twenty-third.

"Well I'm standing on the fucking deck of the fucking ship, see? And I'm looking over the fucking rail at the fucking dock, see? And I says to myself, 'Fuck it! What's a man to do with his fucking self?'

"Then along the fucking dock comes this fucking blonde, see? And she's fucking lovely. So I gives her a fucking smile, and she fucking smiles right back, see? So I says to myself, 'This is fucking good enough for me.'

"So I goes down the fucking gangway to the fucking dock, see? And just as I'm fucking walking up to her, this other bloke fucking walks up, takes her fucking arm, and fucking walks off with her.

"Well, I've got fuck all to do, so I decides to fucking follow them. They goes down the fucking street past the fucking shops, her hanging on to his fucking arm all the way, see? Then they comes to this bit of a fucking park and they turns in, see? So I says to myself, 'Oho! I'll fucking see what he's fucking up to here.'

"So he fucking takes her along this fucking path, and behind some fucking bushes, see? And there's all this fucking giggling and carry-on, see? And while I'm fucking watching, he's giving her the big pash-up, and taking off her fucking clothes — and then — intimacy occurred."

A young boy came before the court charged with stealing a girl's bicycle.

"I didn't steal it, sir," he told the Colonel. "She gave it to me. She was riding me home from school on the handlebars, and she stopped in the woods and took off her blue jeans and her panties, and said I could have anything she had. Well, sir, the panties were girl things, and the blue jeans wouldn't fit me, so I took the bicycle."

The next case was a young woman who complained, "My husband's a sexual monster. I must leave him."

"What do you mean by sexual monster?" asked the Colonel.

"He wants it nearly every night."

"Of course he does. That's what he married you for."

"But he wants it in a most unnatural way."

"Ah. That's different. Tell us about his bestial practices."

"Well, he wants it with the light on."

The following case was not much better. A woman declared, "I demand a divorce. I can't stay with him."

"On what grounds?" asked the Colonel.

"Unreasonable demands. He's wrecking my health with his lusts."

"I see. Now what unreasonable demands? How often?"

"I can't bear to talk about it. It's disgusting."

"Come, Madam. We can't help you if you won't help us. How often?"

"Twice a week."

"Good God almighty," exploded the Colonel. "Women have stood where you're standing now, and called twice a week desertion."

In a group at the football club, one of the players asked a friend who was just back from his honeymoon,

"How's married life, Sid?"

"No bloody good."

They were all too tactful to comment, and quickly changed the subject.

Later the Colonel took the young man aside.

"Look here, Sidney. I couldn't help noticing what you said before — that married life was no good. Now a young fellow just back from his honeymoon should really be thinking that married life is a bit of all right. I don't want to pry, but if you've any problems that you'd like to discuss with an older man, I'll be of any help I can."

"Thanks, Colonel. I've got a problem all right. Do you know we've been married three weeks now and we haven't had sexual intercourse once? Every time I try to put it in she says it hurts too much."

"Ah, yes. Well, Sidney, all you've got to do is, before you start, just drop your cock into a cupful of Vaseline."

Sid stared at him.

"What? Don't tell me you can get yours into a cup!"

One of the Colonel's business operations expanded to the

70

point where he was unable to give it sufficient attention, so he took in a junior partner to share the workload.

The young man in question brought to the enterprise considerable energy and enthusiasm, as well as the latest ideas and methods he had learned in business college.

He initiated a number of changes in routine and operation which made the business more efficient, more productive, and more profitable, and with this the Colonel was very pleased.

The young man, however, the unfortunate habit of claiming for himself all the credit for the success of the business. Such statements as "I've reorganised all the master files so that correspondence will be much easier to locate", "I've closed the Shelby deal, and the contract I signed with him gives us an extra 5 per cent", prompted the Colonel to take him aside.

"Look, old boy. I want you to know I do appreciate all the splendid work you're doing for the firm. But I do wish you would remember that it is still largely my business too. Instead of saying 'I did this', or I sold that', why not say 'We did this', or 'We sold that'? Then it will sound like the partnership it really is."

His words were wasted. His junior partner went on as before. Then, late on afternoon, he came into the Colonel's office, dropped into a chair and announced, "Well! We're in trouble."

The Colonel was so pleased to hear him say "we" instead of "I" that he replied warmly, "My boy, don't worry about it. There's no problem so great we can't solve it if we stick together. This is a partnership after all, isn't it? Now just what is the nature of the trouble that we're in?"

"We've got the typist in the family way."

The Colonel was making his annual tour of inspection of the district old people's home. In the common room he stopped to ask one frail old man, "And how old are you, old man?"

"Eighty-two, Colonel," came the reply in a cracked voice.

"And what's your recipe for a ripe old age, then?"

"Well, Colonel, I believe in no smoking, no drinking, and absolutely nothing to do with women."

The Colonel moved on to another old man and asked the same questions.

"And how old are you, old chap?"

"Eighty-three, Colonel."

"And what's your recipe for a ripe old age?"

"Moderation in all things Colonel. A little bit of smoking, but not too much. A little bit of drinking, but not too much. A little bit of loving, but don't overdo it."

A third resident tottered up to interrupt.

"You don't want to take any notice of these old codgers, Colonel. They don't know what they're talking about. The real secret of a ripe old age is smoking — as much as you want — drinking — whenever you like — and women, women, women!"

"And how old are you?"

"Twenty-four."

In the village there lived, side by side, a Catholic and a Presbyterian. They were good friends, and in the summer-time enjoyed watering their vegetable gardens after tea, and yarning over the fence.

One night the Presbyterian asked his neighbour, "Tell me something. You Catholics aren't supposed to use any form of birth control, while we can use anything at all. And yet you've only got two kids, and we've got five. How do you account for that?"

"Simple," his friend replied, "we use the safe period."

"Safe period? Never heard of it. What's the safe period?"

"Every second Thursday, when you go to Lodge."

The Colonel was carrying an umbrella over his arm when he went into the men's room at the Silver Grill. When he began relieving himself he was accosted by a pansy, who admired his equipment volubly.

"Oh, I say! Isn't it a beauty? Wouldn't you like to give me some?"

"Go away."

"Come on. You know you're really just dying to."

"Go away before I give you a jolly good hiding."

When he turned around the Colonel was amazed to see the

pansy, pants down, facing away, bending over and waving his arse from side to side in a manner that was obviously meant to be provocative.

Taking his umbrella from his arm, the Colonel aimed carefully and shoved it in as far as it would go. The pansy wriggled in ecstasy.

"Oo! Lovely! Lovely!"

"You silly fool! It's my umbrella."

"Well open it. Open it."

A week before the local agricultural show, the Colonel was dismayed to find that his prize bull, which was expected to win at least a blue ribbon, had gone cross-eyed. He sent for the vet.

When the vet arrived, he was quite unruffled. He simply took a length of rubber hose pipe about a yard long, inserted one end in the bull's rectum, and blew forcefully into the other end. The bull's gaze straightaway returned to normal.

Leaving the length of hose pipe behind, the vet went his way, taking with him the Colonel's cheque for £25.

The night before the show, however, the bull again went cross-eyed, and, although the Colonel administered the same treatment, he could get no result. In desperation he again summoned the vet.

"You say you did as I showed you, Colonel?" said the vet. "I can't think why the beast is still cross-eyed, I'm sure. You'd better show me."

The Colonel thrust the hose into the bull's rectum and blew hard through the other end. No result. The vet then took the hose, turned it round, inserted the opposite end, and blowing hard caused the bull's eyes to straighten up at once.

"Did I have the hose round the wrong way, then?" asked the Colonel.

"No," replied the vet. "It makes no difference which way you have it."

"Then why did you turn it round?"

"Well, you don't think I wanted to put that end in my mouth after you'd been sucking it, do you?"

The Colonel stopped his Jaguar outside a country pub and

went inside for a pint or two. There was the usual assortment of local characters in the bar, including a man with a fox terrier dog who was making really fantastic claims as to the speed at which the dog could run. Without wishing to spoil the conviviality of the occasion, the Colonel nevertheless could not help appearing sceptical when the owner claimed that his dog could run at fifty miles an hour, and moreover offered to bet the Colonel £10 that he could do it.

The Colonel accepted the bet and, to settle the matter, he and the owner set off in the Colonel's Jaguar, the Colonel at the wheel, and the owner calling the dog alongside through the open passenger window.

Gradually the Colonel increased speed — ten, twenty, thirty miles an hour — and, amazingly, every time he looked across, the dog appeared to be keeping pace easily.

They had just touched fifty miles an hour when they came to a fork in the road. Unable to decide which road to take, the Colonel applied the brakes suddenly and the car skidded to a halt.

"There you are," said the owner proudly, pointing to the dog alongside the car, "kept pace with us all the way, he did."

"That's remarkable," said the Colonel. "But back at the hotel, your dog wasn't wearing a collar, whereas this one is."

"That's not a collar," declared the owner. "When you put the brakes on, he stopped so fast that his arsehole shot up behind his ears."

Several of the members of the club were having a shot at the Colonel one evening about the fact that he was putting on weight. The Admiral patted him on the tummy and said, "Look at that, Castarse. If it'd been on a woman, I'd say she was pregnant."

The Colonel replied with dignity, "It has been, and she is."

On another occasion the members of the club were discussing their most embarrassing experiences.

The Colonel turned to Ponsonby and said, "What was your most embarrassing experience, Ponsonby?"

"Well, actually, Colonel, it was the time my mother came into my room unexpectedly and caught me playing with myself."

"You mustn't worry too much about that," said the Colonel. "All young fellows do these things from time to time."

"Yes, I know," said Ponsonby. "But this was only last week."

One evening at the club, Ponsonby was telling the Colonel about his experience with the new skin condoms.

"I was told that they were better than rubber — thinner, you know — and they could be washed and used again."

"How did you get on with them?"

"They were all right, you know — thinner and all that — but I did get quite a nasty note from the laundry."

During a game of cards for fairly high stakes, the Colonel was fairly raking it in. At last one of his victims threw down his hand in disgust and left the table. As he passed the Colonel, the loser ran his fingers over the Colonel's bald head.

"My word, Castarse. Your head feels just like my wife's arse."

The Colonel reached up imperturbably and stroked his own bald head.

"By God!" he exclaimed. "So it does."

A Major who had spent many years stationed in remote tropical outposts was telling the members of the Services Club about his ingenious solution for the problem of loneliness.

"I commissioned this painter johnnie to do a life-size painting of a chorus girl. It was a beauty. I had it framed and took it to the Far East with me.

"It was so life-like it was almost better than the real thing. And just in the right place, you know, I bored a hole through the picture.

"After that, whenever I got randy, I used to just bring out the painting and away I'd go. Don't know how I would've got on without it, really."

At the other end of the bar, one of the stewards remarked to the Major's batman, who was also present, "Quite an ingenious fellow, this Major of yours, isn't he?"

The batman grunted. "What the old sod doesn't tell you is

that he always made me bend over behind the painting."

The Major kept badgering poor old Grimes, the steward at the Services Club. Finally, he said to him, "Grimes, do you know that we've got a new nickname for you? We call you Piles. And do you know why? It's because you're such a pain in the arse."

"Indeed, sir. Perhaps you might care to know that the stewards here have a nickname for you, sir. We all call you Virgin."

"Virgin? And me one of the biggest rams in the British Army. And why do you all call me Virgin, then?"

"Because you're an ignorant cunt."

While punting on the Thames, Ponsonby was unlucky enough to lose his pole. He called to a man in a boat with two ladies, "I say, may I borrow one of your oars?"

"Garn with you, you bastard," was the reply. "These ain't 'ores. One of 'em's me muvver, an' the uvver one's me bleedin' sister."

The Colonel entered a suburban railway compartment which was occupied by two men. One of them had a peculiar mannerism, which the Colonel found most distracting. The man kept scratching his elbow again and again.

When at last the sufferer got out at his station, the Colonel remarked to the other man, "Gravely afflicted, your friend."

"Yes indeed. He's got a terrible case of piles."

"I'm not talking about piles," said the Colonel. "I'm talking about all that elbow-scratching just now."

"Yes, that's right. Piles. You see, he's a civil servant and he can't tell his arse from his elbow."

Because of a combination of a slump in business, which greatly reduced the return on the Colonel's investments, and poor seasons in the country, which resulted in very poor crops, there was practically no food in the house. The Colonel had already reduced staff on his country property, and George the footman was also doing the cooking. The Colonel reluctantly instructed George to catch and kill their one and only turkey, which had become almost a family pet, so that they would have something for Sunday dinner.

During the morning the Colonel was passing the kitchen when he became aware of a most unpleasant smell. Locating the source, he was most annoyed to find in the oven the remains of the turkey, burnt to a crisp. He set out to find George, but he was not in any of his usual places. Searching the house systematically he at last found him with Yvette, the French maid, in her room. Yvette was lying on the bed with her legs apart, while George had his head between her legs. This was too much for the Colonel.

"Dammit all, George, this is the limit. First you fuck the only thing we've got to eat, and now you're eating the only thing we've got to fuck."

An American entered a crowded railway carriage, but the only spare seat was occupied by a nasty Alsatian, owned by a big, red-faced woman in hunting tweeds. He asked if the dog might be put on the floor.

"You leave the bloody dog alone," replied the woman.

The unfortunate American searched the train for a seat, without success. He came back and threw the dog out of the window.

The owner appealed to the carriage at large, "Are you all just going to sit there and let this wretched American do that to a gentlewoman?"

The Colonel lowered his *Times* and said, "These Americans do everything back to front, Madam. They eat with the fork in the wrong hand, they drive on the wrong side of the road, and now this fool's thrown out the wrong bitch."

Ponsonby and Carruthers embarked on a business enterprise together in London. In order to make the right contacts they applied for membership of an exclusive country club.

In due course they were advised that their nominations had been accepted and were asked to forward their cheques for £200 each for the first year's subscriptions. Although this was more than they had expected to pay, they felt it would still be worth while because of the extra business they hoped to gain.

After a time they were sent their receipts, along with an invitation to play a round of golf the following Sunday. Packing their clubs in a borrowed sports car they drove down. When they arrived at the club, the Secretary showed them all the facilities and then left them to their own devices.

Near the entrance was a cigar stall. "Do you have any St Andrew's Special Coronas?" Ponsonby asked the attendant.

"Certainly, sir. How many would you like?"

"Half a box, please," he replied, pushing a ten pound note across the counter.

The girl gave him the cigars and returned the note. "There is no charge for these, sir. They are included in your club subscription."

Hearing this, Carruthers decided that he, too, would have a box. They moved into the bar.

"Two whiskies with soda, please," Carruthers asked the steward. When he returned with the tray, Carruthers offered him a fiver.

"The drinks are included in your club subscription, sir, and we are not permitted to accept tips."

After several drinks they moved on to the dining room where they had a splendid luncheon. Their offer to pay for this was met with the standard reply, "It's all included in your subscription."

After they had changed in the locker room, they took their clubs and headed towards the first tee.

They came to the professional's hut. "Do you have any balls?" they asked.

"What brand, sir?"

"I'd like a box of Spalding, please."

"I'll take a box, too, please."

They were moving off when the pro said to them, "Excuse me, gentlemen. That will be twenty-five pounds each."

They paid.

When they were out of earshot, Ponsonby said to Carruthers, "Well at least, old boy, they don't get you by the throat."

Carruthers and Ponsonby picked up a couple of whores and went back to their flat with them. Carruthers was screwing away quite happily when Ponsonby came rushing in from the other bedroom.

"I say, old boy, would you mind very much changing? Mine's my aunt."

On another occasion Carruthers went into a brothel but he did not have much time to spare. As he was unable to make himself heard in the reception area, he lost patience and went into the first room where he found a woman lying on the bed. He spent only five minutes or so with her, then went back to the reception area to settle with the madam.

"Good Lord. Where did you come from?" she asked.

"I've just been in that first room there."

"But the woman in there is dead."

"Is she? I thought she was English."

The Colonel was walking home to his flat one evening when he was hit on the head by a used condom thrown out of an upstairs window. He stormed into the house and demanded to know who was in the room above.

"My daughter," said the owner of the house.

"Is she alone?" asked the Colonel.

"No. My intended son-in-law is with her. Why?"

"No reason. I just thought I ought to tell you that your intended grandson just had a nasty fall."

Two old maids on a train, who had never met before, were having a petty argument about who should sit facing forward and which one of them should have her suitcases on the seat, and so forth. They finally engaged in a pitched battle about whether the window should be open or closed, irritating everyone else in the compartment. The conductor was summoned, but was unable to decide.

"If that window is opened," said one, "I shall catch my death of cold."

"If that window stays shut," insisted the other, "I shall suffocate."

This was too much for the Colonel, who was sitting in the corner.

"Pardon me. May I offer a suggestion?"

The conductor agreed eagerly.

"First, open the window. That will kill one of these bitches. Then shut the window. That will kill the other one. And then we'll all have some peace."

The Colonel suspected his footman of stealing his cigars and shouted to him loudly in the next room, "George! Who's been stealing my cigars?"

No answer. He repeated it more loudly.

Still no answer. He went into the next room and confronted the footman.

"George. Didn't you hear me speaking to you just now?"

"No, sir. There must be something wrong with the acoustics."

"Is that so? Well, you go into the next room and say something, and we'll see whether I can hear it."

The footman went into the next room and shouted at the top of his voice, "Some fat-faced son of a bitch has been screwing hell out of my wife."

He returned to the other room.

"Did you hear me, sir?"

"You're right, George," said the Colonel, red-faced, "I couldn't hear a word. Have a cigar?"

The Colonel was enjoying a drink in Paris with three Frenchmen.

"Tell me," he asked, "what is *sang froid*? I know that if you translate it literally, it means cold blood, but I just don't quite know how the expression is used."

"Well," answered one Frenchman, "let me try to explain. Suppose you 'ave left 'ome — perhaps on a business trip — and you come 'ome unexpectedly. You find your wife in bed with your best friend. You do not get emotional or greatly upset. You smile at them both, and you say, 'Pardon the intrusion.' That is what I would call *sang froid*."

Another of the Frenchmen broke in, "That is not exactly *sang froid*. *Sang froid* is most unusual tact. Suppose in the same situation you wave 'ello to your wife and your friend who are in bed, and very casually you say, 'Pardon the intrusion, sir. Don't mind me. Please continue.' Now that is what I would call *sang froid*."

"Ah, perhaps," said the third. "But for me *sang froid* is more than this. If in the same situation you said, 'Pardon the intrusion; please continue,' and your best friend in bed could continue, then that is what I would call *sang froid*."

After a weekend house party, the Colonel was saying goodbye to his host at the railway station.

"And I specially want to thank you for the use of your wife. She was more fun in bed than any woman I ever knew."

After the train pulled out, another traveller, who had overheard this, said to the Colonel, "How on earth could you say a thing like that?"

"Well I had to," said the Colonel. "She wasn't really much good, but I didn't want to hurt his feelings."

# RENEWED HOSTILITIES

Before his second marriage, the Colonel visited a physician.

"What seems to be the trouble, Colonel?"

"No trouble, doctor. It's just that I'm about to get married again and I wondered if you would have any advice for me."

"How old are you, Colonel?"

"Sixty."

"And who's the bride-to-be?"

"The Lady Margaret Templeton."

The doctor knew the Lady Margaret Templeton. She was twenty-three.

"About the only advice that I can give you is to take in a lodger."

The Colonel thought this was rather odd, but said nothing. He did not see the doctor again until they met in the street about five months later.

"How's the wife, Colonel?"

"She's pregnant."

"Splendid. And how's the lodger?"

"Oh, she's pregnant too."

On the Colonel's wedding night, he confronted his bride, stripped to the buff.

"Now," he said, "let's get a few things straight. Do you know what this is?" he asked, pointing.

"Yes," she said, "that's a wee-wee."

"No it's not. It's a prick. From now on we call that a prick."

"Oh no," she said, "I've seen pricks before. That's definitely a wee-wee."

When the Colonel was married, because he was such a keen rugby enthusiast, the marriage had to take place on a Friday so that he could see the big game the next day. On Saturday evening after the game he was in his usual place at the football club bar.

Several of the younger members took the opportunity to have a shot at the Colonel about his recent marriage.

"How's married life, Colonel?"

"What's it feel like to be getting it regularly again?"

"What was the score last night, Colonel?"

"Yes. What was the score last night?"

The Colonel replied modestly, "Well actually, thirteen."

"Thirteen?" they repeated in disbelief.

"Yes, thirteen," said the Colonel, "but of course four of them were unconverted tries."

On their honeymoon the Colonel and his bride stopped for several nights at a charming wayside inn. Their room on the first floor gave them an excellent view of the grounds, and of all the farm animals the innkeeper kept.

Before each meal the innkeeper's wife would knock on their door and call out, "Would you like to have some lunch?" or "Would you like to have some dinner?"

Not wishing to be interrupted the Colonel would always call out, "No thanks. We're living on the fruits of love."

On the third day it was the innkeeper himself who mounted the stairs and knocked.

"Would you like to have some lunch?"

"No thanks, old boy. We're living on the fruits of love."

"Well I wish you'd stop throwing the skins out of the window. They're choking my ducks.

The Colonel went to the Vicar privately to seek his advice.

"Look here, old chap. I've done something I don't think I should have, and I want to know whether I'm likely to be thrown out of the Church."

"What sort of thing?"

"Well, it's like this. We've only been married a few weeks, as you know. The other day I came up behind my wife as she was bending down and — I don't know what came over me — I let her have it. Just like that. Bang. Will I be thrown out of the Church?"

"Well, now. The Church does not actually condone behaviour of that sort, but at the same time you are in the married state, and so do enjoy certain rights and privileges.

No. You won't be thrown out of the Church.

"What made you think you'd be thrown out of the Church anyway?"

"Well, we were thrown out of Harrods."

Not long after their marriage, the Colonel came home after a day at the office to find his young wife stretched languorously on the sofa, dressed in a revealing negligée.

"Guess what I've got planned for dinner," she cooed seductively. "And don't tell me you had it for lunch."

Before returning home from a trip, the Colonel made his way to a department store to buy his wife a homecoming present.

"I should like to buy my wife a silk nightgown, trimmed with fur at the bottom."

"I'm sorry, sir. We have an excellent range of silk nightgowns, but none of them has the fur trimming at the hem. It's most unusual. Why do you need it?"

The Colonel smiled. "To keep my wife's neck warm."

Her ladyship had just slipped into her gown when James opened the door of her room, unannounced, and entered. She was taken aback by his sudden entrance. Suppose he had come in half a minute earlier, when she only had on her scanty underwear? She took him to task so that he would not repeat the offence.

"James. Don't you know that you should knock on the door before coming into my room? I might be undressed."

James smiled blandly.

"Your ladyship has nothing to worry about," he reassured her. "Before I come in, I always look through the keyhole."

Her ladyship was examining herself in a new petticoat in the bedroom mirror.

"Does it look all right?" she asked the Colonel.

"It looks very nice," said the Colonel, "but your pants are coming down."

She glanced anxiously at the mirror.

"No they're not."

"Oh, yes they are," said the Colonel. "I've made up my mind."

Her ladyship hired an old Jewish painter to redecorate their London flat. He painted the bedroom, bathroom and hallway, and then left for the day. When the Colonel came home, her ladyship told him how pleased she was with the old man's work. The Colonel grunted with approval.

"Is the paint dry?"

As he spoke he touched the wall and left finger marks on the surface. Her ladyship had a few words to say about clumsiness.

Next morning the old painter returned, and began mixing the colour for the living room. Her ladyship came in and said, "Before you start, come into the bedroom. I want to show you where my husband put his hand last night."

The old man looked at her sheepishly.

"Please, lady. I'm an old man. More helpful it would be if you gave me better a glass of tea."

Early in their marriage the Colonel and her ladyship were receiving guests at their country estate. The Colonel excused himself briefly to choose the wine for dinner, and when he returned to the drawing room was amazed to find everyone leaving in a great huff.

When they were alone he said to her ladyship, "What happened, my dear?"

"I don't know," she replied through her tears. "They were talking about rats in country houses, and someone said the best way to get rid of them was to pound broken glass in their holes. So I asked, 'But how do you get the rats to stand still long enough?'"

The Colonel would sometimes play golf with her ladyship. One day her fifteen-year-old niece who was visiting walked round with them. At one point the Colonel was disgusted to miss a six-inch putt and exclaimed, "Oh, fuck."

Her ladyship rebuked him, but the Colonel looked at her niece, her full bust, round bottom and red lips.

"Surely you must have heard that expression before?" he asked.

"Yes, Uncle, but not spoken in anger."

Before she went into hospital to have her baby, the Colonel's wife reminded him a number of times that when the baby was born he was to put the correct birth notice in the newspaper.

Later, when he visited her and his baby son, one of the first things she asked him was, "Did you put the birth announcement in the paper?"

"I did. And a pretty penny it cost, too. Five hundred and seventy pounds."

"Why was it so much?"

"I don't know. I gave the girl the wording just as you told me, and when she asked me, 'How many insertions?' I told her, 'Twice a day for twelve months'."

Soon after the arrival of his son, the Colonel paraded the whole regiment.

"Officers, non-commissioned officers, and men of the Thirty-ninth Royal Loamshires. I have called you together to make a special announcement. This morning my wife gave birth to a fine baby boy weighing eight pounds. Officers, non-commissioned officers, and men of the Thirty-ninth Royal Loamshire Regiment, I thank you, one and all."

The Colonel insisted that the boy be circumcised in accordance with family tradition. Soon after he visited the hospital. First he saw the matron.

"I say, matron, how's my wife today?"

"She's doing very well, Colonel."

"And what about my son, eh?"

"Well, he had an upset tummy so we gave him a teaspoon of brandy. He seems all right now."

"Will it be in order if I go in and see them?"

"Certainly, Colonel. Your wife is giving him his feed just now."

The Colonel entered the ward and was confronted with the touching spectacle of his young wife sitting up in bed with his baby son at the breast. He absorbed this delightful tableau in silence for a moment, then observed, "It's easy to see he's a Castarse. Only a week old and already he's in bed with a beautiful woman, his mouth full of tit, his belly full of brandy, and a sore cock."

Not long before her ladyship's confinement, one of the men in the village had just finished building a new house and invited the neighbours in for a drink to celebrate.

Many of the guests made quite flattering remarks about the house, but the wife modestly replied, "Many men in the village assisted my husband, so he cannot claim all the credit."

The Colonel had been very impressed with the woman's humility and praised her highly to her ladyship, saying that to be successful a man needed such a mate. Her ladyship had pouted with anger and jealousy, but had said nothing.

After he brought his wife and son home from the hospital, the Colonel invited all his neighbours in to celebrate. When she was complimented on the happy event, her ladyship replied, "Many men in the village co-operated in bringing this about, so my husband cannot claim all the credit."

A batch of young officers, fresh from Officer Training School, were arriving to take up their posts in the Colonel's regiment. Accordingly, the Colonel arranged a reception for them so that they could meet the other officers and their wives.

When the night came, the Colonel searched among the crowd for his own wife. At last he said to his batman, "I say, Prendergast, where's my wife?"

"Her ladyship is sorry, sir. She's unable to come."

"Unable to come? Why on earth not?"

"She's in bed with cramp, sir."

"Cramp? Cramp? He's not even a member of the regiment."

As his son grew up, the Colonel delighted in taking a continuing interest in his progress. The young fellow showed every sign of being a chip off the old block.

One day the Colonel's son was visiting the zoo with his parents. Seeing the elephant with an enormous erection, he asked his mother what it was.

"It's nothing," she said. "Shhh!"

Not satisfied, the boy turned to his father and asked the same question.

"Why don't you ask your mother?"

"I did ask her. She said it's nothing."

"That's the trouble with your mother. She's been spoiled."

On another occasion at the zoo, the family watched the monkeys for a time. The boy asked his father, "How long does it take to make a baby monkey?"

"About six months," the Colonel replied.

"Well then, why are they in such an awful hurry?"

The Colonel was in the bedroom with her ladyship, changing. He had just removed his tweeds and undershorts when their young son walked in.

"Mummy," he cried, pointing to his father's disproportionately ample endowment, "what's that?"

"It's ... well, it's Daddy's secret weapon," she told him.

"If it weren't for that, young man, you wouldn't be here in this room now. And, come to think of it, neither would I."

Her ladyship's niece stayed the night at the Colonel's London flat for she was to be presented at a debutante ball; the Colonel himself was out of town. She did not return from the ball until 3 a.m. and then woke up very late to find James, the butler, standing by her bed with black coffee.

"James, how did I come to be in this bed?"

"You came home very late, and very tired, my lady."

"But James, I'm undressed, and in my nightgown."

"I couldn't let you spoil your good evening clothes, my lady."

"Good Lord, James. Do you mean that you undressed me and put me to bed without my knowing it?"

"Yes, my lady."

"James, tell the truth. Was I tight?"

"Not after the first time, my lady."

The Colonel and her ladyship were giving a large party, and they ran short of caviare. Her ladyship told James to replace it with lead shot and butter. He did so without the guests noticing the substitution. One woman, indeed, commented on its excellence and kept coming back for more.

After the guests had left, the woman returned, very apologetic, and said to her ladyship, "Look, I'm frightfully sorry, but I dropped my purse in your garden, and when I bent down to pick it up, I shot your cat."

A woman at the party was startled to find herself seized and embraced by a male guest who was very much under the weather. But he soon released her and apologised.

"Excuse me, my dear. I thought you were my wife."

The woman quickly recovered and said acidly, "Fancy having you for a husband, you drunken, clumsy, disgusting beast!"

The man grinned. "There you are," he said. "You not only look like her, you sound like her, too."

The Colonel was telling his friends at the club how his five-year-old son got the maid pregnant.

"But that's impossible," protested the Admiral.

"Indeed it's not," said the Colonel. "The little wretch punctured all my condoms with a pin."

Her ladyship was given as a present a pedigreed black chow-chow dog, and got such satisfactory fees for its stud services that she began faking the dog's documents so that the dog gave far more services than it should have to produce good results.

She usually fed the dog on canned dog food, but would give him fresh chopped steak or fish cakes after every service, saying, "Here's your share, darling."

Unfortunately the dog couldn't keep up the pace, and died.

Telling the Colonel about it, her ladyship said, "I must've cut it too fine. Just when things were going beautifully, the damned dog fucked himself to death."

Her ladyship was entertaining the vicar. Just as she was pouring out the vicar's tea, a cat came screaming through the

parlour and leapt out of the bay window. Right after it, in hot pursuit, came young Castarse.

He stopped in the middle of the parlour and announced, "If I catch that cat, I'll fuck it," and then dived out of the window after it.

"He will, too," said her ladyship. "He's a horny little bastard. More cream?"

About this time, her ladyship sought advice from her physician.

"It's my husband, the Colonel. I don't think he cares about me as much as he used to when we were first married. How can I discover whether there is another woman?"

"What makes you think your husband has lost interest in you?" asked the doctor.

"Well, when we were first married, about six years ago, he used to make love to me all the time. Sometimes several times in one night."

"And now?"

"Now it's only occasionally. As little as once a fortnight. I'm sure there must be someone else."

"Perhaps we shouldn't be too hasty in drawing conclusions, your ladyship. How old is the Colonel now?"

"Sixty-seven"

"That may be your answer then. As a man advances in years, he tends to become less amorous."

He scribbled busily on a pad.

"Have these pills made up. When you have a suitable occasion, slip one into his cocktail before dinner. I think you'll find they'll do the trick."

In less than a week her ladyship was in the surgery again, if possible even more distressed than the last time.

"Did the little pink pills do their job?" the doctor asked.

"Only too well."

"Tell me what happened."

"We were about to have dinner. I did just as you said, and slipped a pill into his drink. Then, before I could stop him, he seized the table cloth and tossed everything on the floor. He threw me on the table, tore off my panties, and made passionate love to me as though he'd never seen a woman before."

"Ah, yes. Unconventional, but effective. But what is the nature of your difficulty now?"

"Oh, doctor! How can we ever hope to reserve another table at Claridge's?"

The Colonel became suspicious of the fact that her ladyship was playing golf every day, and asked James to keep an eye on her. James reported that she really spent her time in the woods with the handsome young golf pro.

"How long do you think this has been going on?" the Colonel asked.

"Well, sir. Judging from the freckles on his arse, I'd say it's been going on all summer."

Her ladyship was talking to one of her friends in the city one day and asked, "And what about your niece, Felicity? What is she doing now?"

"Oh, Felicity has just become engaged to the loveliest boy."

"Really? And what does he do?"

"He's an officer in the Burmese Army."

"I see. And is he coloured?"

"No. Only their privates are coloured."

"Really? How exotic."

Felicity made herself a dress with a Chinese collar and when it was complete, decided that all it needed to set it off was to work some Chinese characters down from one shoulder. To make them look authentic, she copied some suitable characters from the front of a Chinese restaurant.

When she wore the dress, however, she was dismayed that any young Chinese men she saw would at once burst out laughing.

Finally, she asked a Chinese girl student to translate the writing on her dress.

The girl said, "It says, 'Cheap but delicious'."

An elderly lady was horrified when she came upon the Colonel's son in a quiet corner smoking a cigar.

"Little boys shouldn't smoke," she admonished sternly.

Young Castarse was unruffled.

"I was smoking cigarettes when I was eight," he told her.

The old lady was even more horrified.

"Even so," she said, "it's still wrong for someone so young to smoke."

"That's nothing," scoffed the lad. "I had my first affair with a little girl when I was six."

"Who was this little girl?"

"I really don't know. I was drunk at the time."

The Colonel was on a hunting trip in Switzerland and stayed the night at a chalet which seemed to be otherwise deserted. He chose a room on the ground floor just inside the main entrance and, after cooking and eating an evening meal, before retiring sat down on the bed to clean his rifle.

Due to an oversight the weapon was still loaded and discharged a shot which fortunately missed him, the bullet passing through the ceiling.

After breakfast he returned the key to the concierge, who asked him, "Monsieur! Last night you 'ave the accident with your rifle, yes?"

"Oh, yes. Damn thing went off when I was cleaning it, but there was no harm done. Lucky thing there was no one else about, or it would've given them a nasty start."

"But, Monsieur, there was someone else about. In the room above you was an English 'oneymoon couple. Your bullet shot the young man's finger off."

"Oh, I say. How awful — my apologies to the young man. But what a bit of luck it wasn't a Frenchman. I would've blown his brains out."

One Christmas the Colonel gave his young hopeful, who was seven at the time, a diary. The lad was so pleased he could hardly wait until New Year to start filling its pages.

On the fourth of January he asked his mother, "Where did I come from, Mother?"

Not being prepared for a long discussion she replied, "Oh, the gardener found you one morning in the rose garden."

The lad seemed satisfied, but later in the day caught his grandmother alone and asked her, "Grandma, where did Mother come from?"

The old lady replied, "Oh, the gardener found her one morning in the rose garden."

Great Grandmother was still alive at the time, so the boy went to her room and asked her, "Nanna, where did Grandmother come from?"

In a cracked voice came the reply, "Oh, the gardener found her one morning in the rose garden."

That night, in the privacy of his room, young Castarse filled in his diary before going to bed. For 4 January he made the following entry:

"Insofar as I have been able to ascertain, there has been no sexual relationship on my mother's side of the family for three generations."

When he was still seven, the Colonel's son confided to him that he was in love with Patricia, the little girl next door, and that they planned to be married.

The Colonel hid his amusement and asked in all seriousness, "What are you going to do about money?"

"I have my pocket money," replied the boy, "and Patricia has nearly ten shillings saved up."

"That's all right for now," said the Colonel, "but what will you do when you have children?"

"Well, we've had pretty good luck so far."

The Colonel was walking along the seashore with his son when the lad was quick enough to grab the end of a worm and pull it out of its hole.

The Colonel said to the boy, "I'll give you ten shillings if you can put it back."

The boy tried unsuccessfully for some time and then asked if he might have half an hour. He took the worm away. When he reappeared the worm was stiff and he slid it straight into the hole.

"How did you do that, my boy?" asked the Colonel.

"It was easy," said the lad. "I just sprayed it with mother's hairspray until it went all stiff."

The Colonel rewarded the boy with ten shillings.

Next morning he again sought the boy out. "You know that business of yours with the hair spray? Well here's ten shillings for you."

"But, Father, you gave me ten shillings yesterday."

"I know. I know," said the Colonel. "This one's from your mother.

"Daddy must be going to buy a really small, compact car," announced the Colonel's son at breakfast.

"Why do you think that, dear?" asked his mother.

"Because I just found a tiny inner tube in his coat pocket."

Her ladyship had been displaying herself in various rather expensive new dresses, but the Colonel refrained from asking her how she had managed to buy them out of her housekeeping allowance in case it brought on another row about how mean he was. But when her ladyship appeared wearing a brand new silver mink jacket, he was moved to ask her how she came by it.

"Oh, the most exciting thing happened, dear. I won it in a raffle at the tennis club."

The next week she was wearing a new pair of diamond earrings. He enquired how she got them.

"I won them in a raffle at the golf club. Actually, I want to dash out again in a few minutes to another raffle reception. Be a darling and run a bath for me."

"Well, my love," replied the Colonel. "I'm not too sure that you ought to take a bath just now."

"Why on earth not?"

"Well, dear, we don't want you to get your raffle ticket wet, do we?"

The Colonel came home unexpectedly from grouse shooting to find her ladyship in bed with a neighbouring member of the landed gentry. In a rage, the Colonel summoned James and demanded his pistol. The butler dutifully produced it, and handed the weapon to the seething Colonel.

The Colonel took careful aim at the adulterer, but James interrupted the shot, advising, "Do the sporting thing, sir. Shoot him on the rise."

An economic recession had got the Colonel down. He said to his wife, "You know, if you would learn how to cook, we could do without the maid."

"Perhaps we could," she replied, "and if you would learn how to fuck, we could do without the chauffeur."

Young Castarse arrived late for school one morning and excused himself by saying that he had had to take the bull to the cow.

"But couldn't your father have done that?" asked the teacher.

"No, Miss, you have to have a bull."

The lad asked his mother one day, "Mother do people go to heaven feet first?"

"Why no, dear," she replied. "Why do you ask?"

"Well the maid was lying on the bed with her feet up, shouting, 'Oh God, I'm coming!' and she would've too, if Father hadn't been holding her down."

On another occasion he told his mother that his father could take a WAF apart. When she asked how he knew, he ex-

plained that he had heard the Colonel telling Uncle Ponsonby
how the night before he had screwed the arse off a WAF.

James said to the Colonel one day, "I'm afraid, sir, that I
must tender my resignation."

"Resignation? That's impossible, James. Why, you've been
with me man and boy now for twenty-two years. What's the
reason?"

"I'd rather not say, sir."

"Come on, man. Is it her ladyship?"

"Well, yes, sir."

"What happened?"

"Well, sir, yesterday, as I was on the upstairs landing, her
ladyship called out to me from her bedroom, 'James!' I went
to the door and said, 'Yes madam.'

"She called me over to the bed, 'James,'" she said.

"I went over and she was entirely nude, sir, if you take my
meaning. I said 'Yes, madam.'

"She said, 'James, do you fuck?'

"I said, 'Yes madam.'

"She said, 'Well fuck off, it's April Fool's Day'."

Coming home in the early hours rather sozzled, the Colonel
tiptoed in so as not to wake her ladyship. Just as he closed the
door the cuckoo-clock cuckooed twice. He thought
suddenly, "Oh damn. She'll hear that, and know what time I
turned in."

So he himself cuckooed ten more times and made his way
to bed. Her ladyship asked, "You're late, dear, aren't you?"

The Colonel said, "Yes, the clock struck twelve as I came
upstairs."

"That reminds me," her ladyship replied, "we must get that
clock seen to. I heard it cuckoo twice, and then it said, 'Oh
shit!', farted, and then cuckooed the other ten."

The Colonel appeared in the surgery of the local doctor
with a steel-shafted golf club wrapped around his neck. The
doctor was most concerned.

"I'll get it off for you, of course, but how in the name of

goodness did you get it there in the first place?"

"Well, you see, I was playing golf yesterday with the wife, and at one stage she lost her ball. We looked everywhere for it — on the fairway, in the rough. Then I noticed this cow lying to one side. I walked around it, and lifted up its tail. And there, by Jove, was a golf ball. So I called out to the wife, 'Over here, dear. This looks like yours'."

Young Castarse said to his mother one afternoon, "Mother, guess what I saw Father and the maid doing on the bed?"

"Not now," she said. Then, after a moment's reflection, she added, "You wait until Mother asks you."

At dinner that night with the Colonel she said, "Now, son, what were you going to tell me this afternoon?"

"Oh, nothing," said the boy. "Only that I saw Father and the maid on the bed together, doing just what you and Uncle Percy used to do last summer when Father was away shooting."

The lad was playing in the back yard when his mother saw him lose his temper and kick a chicken.

"Just for that," she said, "you don't get any eggs for two weeks."

Later the boy lost his temper again and kicked the dog.

"Just for that," said his mother, "you don't get any hot dogs for two weeks."

Not long afterwards the Colonel came home in a fine old temper and kicked the cat. The boy looked at her ladyship.

"Well, Mother, are you going to tell him or shall I?"

Her ladyship approached the Colonel one day and said, "Since our son Reginald is approaching manhood, I think that the time has come for you to tell him about . . . well, you know . . . about the birds and bees."

Accordingly, the Colonel took the young man aside that evening.

"My boy," he said, "do you remember the special training session that I arranged for you with my very good friend Mademoiselle Collette?"

"Oh I should say so, Father. Yes indeed."

"Well your mother wants you to know that the birds and the bees do the same thing."

Going into the cellar one day, her ladyship caught the Colonel screwing the servant girl. There was a fine old scene.

A short time after, finding that Mary was packing her boxes to leave, she enquired the reason.

"I couldn't think of stopping, your ladyship, not after what you saw in the cellar."

"Go along with you, girl," said her ladyship. "Do you think I mind? Perhaps with what you do in the cellar, and I do upstairs, between us we may keep the old whoremonger at home."

The Colonel was warned by his doctor that he was undermining his health by making love several times every day, and warned him that he would die very soon unless he stopped.

The doctor met the Colonel some weeks later, obviously much worse, and said to him, "Are you taking my advice? You know — limiting it to once each day?"

"Don't you worry," replied the Colonel, "I'm keeping track of every one."

He consulted a notebook. "The last one was for the second Monday in August, 1998."

When he was ten, young Castarse announced to his mother that he had just had his first naughty. Next morning she was in tears as she told the Colonel. He reached for a heavy frying pan.

"Don't hit him, dear," she cried, "it's really all our own fault."

"Hit him?" said the Colonel. "I'm not going to hit him. I'm going to cook him some steak and eggs. He can't keep that up on corn flakes."

The Joneses were social climbers and when they moved into a select part of the country they invited some of their more superior neighbours in for an evening of bridge. They carefully prepared everything, then packed their twelve-year-old son off to bed and settled down for a pleasant evening.

Unfortunately Junior misbehaved. He kept coming downstairs ... he couldn't sleep ... his leg hurt ... he wanted water. There was one interruption after another.

At last the host and hostess appealed to the Colonel.

"Yes," he said. "I can quieten him. Someone take my hand for ten minutes and leave the rest to me."

So saying, he took Junior upstairs.

The rest of the evening was perfect and not a sound was heard from the lad. As the guests departed, Mrs Jones thanked the Colonel profusely and asked him what the secret was.

"It was nothing really, Madam. I simply taught him to masturbate."

The Colonel's son was still in his early teens when he marched into the local brothel, waving a ten pound note, and demanded of the madam, "Give me a girl who's got syphilis."

"You dreadful boy," she replied. "Fancy saying a thing like that. All my girls are clean."

"It's no good," he persisted. "I want a girl with syphilis."

"In heaven's name what for?"

"I want to catch it so I can give it to the housemaid."

"My God! What kind of a monster are you? What have you got against the poor girl?"

"Nothing. But she'll give it to Dad, and he'll give it to Mum, and she'll give it to the parish priest — and he's the bastard I'm really after."

One day the Colonel was going through his son's books of account and called the boy's attention to several items.

| | |
|---|---|
| Present for Lady Millicent | 50 pounds |
| Present for Lady Julia | 75 pounds |
| Present for Lady Margaret | 60 pounds |

"Look here, son," he began, "You're paying far too much for your sex. And in the second place, you might put the entries down in your accounts more discreetly, say shooting, ten pounds or shooting, fifteen pounds."

Some weeks later the Colonel was again going through his son's accounts, and was gratified to find,

|            |                        |
|------------|------------------------|
| Shooting   | 10 pounds              |
| Shooting   | 12 pounds 10 shillings |
| Shooting   | 3 pounds               |

and then he came to,

| Repairs to gun | 150 pounds. |
|----------------|-------------|

The Colonel told the maid that he would be taking his family away for a week.

"The man for the artificial breeding is coming today to inseminate one of the cows. I've put a big nail in the window frame by the right cow. You just show him when he gets here."

Later in the day the artificial inseminator arrived. The maid took him to the barn, and pointed to the cow.

"That's the one."

"How do you know?" he asked.

"By that big nail the Colonel hammered into the window frame."

"What's that for then?"

"To hang your pants on, I suppose. Can I watch?"

Before leaving, the Colonel also gave careful instructions to the maid as to how she should handle any enquiries during his absence.

"Now, Polly, if anyone should want the services of the bull, the charge is 50 pounds. If they need the hog or the ram, it will cost them 35 pounds. Is that clear?"

She repeated the prices to him and, satisfied that she understood, the Colonel departed.

The following morning, Polly was visited by farmer Giles.

"Where's the Colonel?"

"Away for a few days. He's left me in charge. Can I be of help?"

"I really wanted to see the Colonel. That son of his has got my young daughter in the family way."

"Yes, you'd better see the Colonel himself. I don't know how much he'll charge you for that."

A titled lady who was a guest at one of the Colonel's parties came to him, very indignant.

"Your wife, Colonel. She just practically told me I was a woman of the streets."

"Don't think any more about it, my dear," he replied. "I've been retired from the Army for ten years, and she still calls me Colonel."

In the whorehouse the elderly Colonel would not take any girl but Mary, who happened to be occupied at the time.

The madam asked, "But what has Mary got that the rest of my girls don't have?"

The Colonel sighed. "Patience."

During a routine examination, the doctor asked the Colonel, "How's your sex life these days, Colonel?"

"Quite good, doctor, quite good. Except during June and July."

"You give it up during the summer, then?"

"It's not that," replied the Colonel, "it's just that my man James has his holidays then and I've got no one to lift me on and off."

The Colonel and her ladyship were on a cruise to the Far East. For the Colonel it was mainly a rest cure and he spent most of the time flat on his back on a bunk in their cabin, fast asleep.

Not so her ladyship. Every port that the ship put into she would go ashore and head for the native bazaars where she would buy all manner of exotic curios.

In one of the bazaars she saw a snake charmer with a little flute charm a snake out of a basket until it was standing nearly straight up in the air. This gave her an idea.

She asked the snake charmer what he would take for his little flute. At first the man was reluctant to part with it, but after some bargaining they settled on a price and soon her

ladyship was hurrying back to the ship with her purchase.

She went straight down to the cabin and found the Colonel, as usual, flat on his back fast asleep. Softly she began to play on the little flute.

Soon the bedclothes began to rise, and as she kept playing, they kept rising until they were more than a foot above the Colonel.

Delighted, she slipped off her clothes and threw back the covers to find, standing on its end, the cord of the Colonel's pyjama pants.

The Colonel was back in London for some weeks before he met Ponsonby.

"Where have you been?" he asked. "I haven't seen you for weeks."

"In jail," Ponsonby replied.

"In jail? What for?"

"Well, about eight weeks ago I was standing on a corner when a beautiful young girl rushed up with a policeman and said, 'He's the man, officer. He's the one who assaulted me'. And, you know, I felt so flattered, I admitted it."

The Colonel telephoned his wife from a banquet to which he had been invited.

"You know, my dear, there's something very unexpected here. I thought it would be just drinking and speeches, but there are naked girls dancing on the tables, and they're going under the tables with the men. What should I do?"

"If you think you can do anything," replied her ladyship, "come straight home."

At great expense the Colonel obtained a box of Elixir of Youth tablets, but instead of taking one each night, he downed the whole box at bedtime.

Next morning his family had great difficulty waking him. After their efforts had continued for more than a quarter of an hour he was heard to mumble, "Very well. I'll get up. But I'm not going to school."

The Colonel visited the doctor with an unusual complaint.

He was afraid that something was radically wrong with him. He told the doctor that the first time he made love, he felt good, warm and comfortable all over. But the second time it was different. He felt cold, and shivered so much that his teeth sometimes chattered.

The doctor had never come across a condition like this before and gave the Colonel a complete physical examination. He was unable to find anything wrong with him and asked him to send his wife in for a consultation.

When she arrived, the physician advised her that he had examined her husband, found him to be in fairly good shape, yet he had complained of very odd symptoms.

"He tells me that the first time he makes love to you, he's warm and comfortable, but the next time, he's so cold that he actually shivers."

"And why not?" asked her ladyship with derision. "The first time is in July. The next time it's in December."

Her ladyship was driving past Buckingham Palace in the Daimler when she was struck by the fine figure of a guardsman — a strapping specimen of manhood. She had the chauffeur stop nearby and ask the guard if he'd like to spend the weekend with the lady in the car. The guardsman stood stiffly to attention and did not take the slightest notice.

Her ladyship had the chauffeur drive right alongside the guard and said to him herself, "Come to my place in the country and the car's yours."

Still she got no reply and drove away, thinking, "I'll get him somehow."

Next day she appeared in the Rolls and said to the guardsman when she was close enough, "One night with me and the Rolls is yours, and almost anything else you'd like, to go with it."

The guardsman was today marking time, and without breaking step he replied, "Madam! I'll have you know that I am a Viscount, of noble lineage of the greatest antiquity. I have money, a castle, three country estates, two town houses, and properties in Portugal and Brazil. I have two Rolls-Royces, a sports car, a hunter and a yacht. I don't know what you want, but if anyone wants fucking it's me, for getting drunk one afternoon and signing up for this bloody guardsman business."

The Colonel and her ladyship were consummating their silver wedding anniversary.

"Put it in," said her ladyship.

"It is in," said the Colonel.

"No it's not. Put it in."

"I tell you it is in."

"And I tell you it's not."

"There's only one way to settle this. James!"

James made his appearance in the doorway.

"You called, sir?"

"Yes, James. I want you to settle a little difference of opinion between her ladyship and me. I say I'm in, but her Ladyship says I'm not. Have a look like a good chap and tell us who's right."

James approached the bed and made a close appraisal of the situation.

"Well, James?"

"Well, sir, actually you're both right."

"Both right? What do you mean?"

"Well, sir, the middle is in, but neither of the ends are."

Her ladyship picked up an out-of-work tramp and took him home because he had very large shoes on, and she had been told that men with big feet have big pricks. She gave him a steak dinner with plenty of pepper and beer, and dragged him off to bed.

In the morning the man woke up alone to find a ten pound note on the mantelpiece with a brief note.

"Buy yourself a pair of shoes that fit you."

The Colonel was making a train journey in the company of a young nurse who was looking after him during a particularly bad attack of bronchitis. He did not have much to say to her, but the journey was punctuated from time to time by the Colonel's severe bouts of coughing.

The only other person in the compartment with them was a young commercial traveller who had had quite a few ales with his confreres before catching the train. Wincing every time the Colonel coughed, and cowering under the Colonel's glare, the young man was daydreaming about how much he would enjoy a bottle of oysters. Imagine his surprise when his gaze wandered to the rack above the Colonel's head and he saw the very thing.

Soon after this the train plunged into a long tunnel and the traveller took advantage of the darkness to take the bottle from the rack, pull the cork, and drink the entire contents. He was back in his seat before the train emerged from the tunnel.

Just then the Colonel started to cough once again. Turning to his nurse he barked, "Nurse! Pass me down my phlegm bottle."

In the club one night, the Colonel and the Admiral were discussing the news that men were so scarce in Paris that the women were paying 20 pounds a night to gigolos.

"But who can live on 20 pounds a month?"

Carruthers and the Colonel were reminiscing about the war.

"Colonel, do you remember during the First War, when we were in France, how they used to put saltpetre in our coffee to stop us from thinking about women?"

"Yes. Why?"

"It's just beginning to work on me."

The Colonel had enjoyed good health nearly all his life, but now he told the doctor that he was feeling decidedly peculiar. After a cursory examination, and some preliminary tests, the doctor told the Colonel that he would have to take more tests because he appeared to have either venereal disease, or the measles.

The Colonel returned to the surgery the following day for the results of the tests. The doctor told him, "I'm afraid I have bad news for you. It's V.D."

"Of course it is," said the Colonel, "where would I come in contact with the measles?"

The Colonel confided in the doctor. "I think I must be becoming impotent."

"Really? When did you first notice any symptoms?"

"Well, last night, and then again this morning."

"Well, I'm afraid there's not much I can do for you. You're much too old for this sort of thing."

"Well then, Doctor, could you give me something to take the ideas out of my mind?"

As he walked along the street, the Colonel came across a small boy sitting on a doorstep crying his heart out.

"What's the matter, son?" he asked kindly. "What are you crying about?"

The boy replied, "I'm crying because I can't do what· the big boys do."

Whereupon the Colonel sat down beside him and began crying too.

Although he was approaching eighty, the Colonel refused to accept his loss of sexual desire and stamina. Again he consulted the doctor.

The doctor was amused and asked, "Why should you be so concerned? It's only to be expected at your time of life."

"But a friend of mine who is eighty-five says he still makes love to his wife every night."

The doctor smiled. "Why can't you say the same thing?"

The Colonel was alone in an hotel room watching television. There came a knock at the door. On opening it, a shapely, beautiful young girl walked in.

"Oh, I'm sorry," she said. "I must be in the wrong room."

"No, you're in the right room, my dear. You're just thirty years too late."

In the club one night the ageing Colonel was having a few drinks with the Admiral and several others when the Admiral remarked, "By George! When you see some of these young things today in their mini-skirts and bikinis and what-not it makes you want to take them on your knee and cuddle them and kiss them."

"Yes," said the Colonel reflectively, "but wasn't there something else we used to do, too?"

The Colonel fell ill and the three attending physicians agreed that he was suffering from a very bad case of colitis. His stomach could not retain anything. They decided in consultation that the patient would have to be fed rectally.

In the afternoon the Admiral called to enquire about the Colonel's health. James conveyed the dismal facts. The Admiral said that he would call again later in the week. A few days later he asked James about the patient's progress.

"Much better," he was informed. "Though he's still being fed rectally, his disposition is greatly improved. It would have done your heart good today to see how his arsehole snapped at a piece of buttered toast."

In his old age the Colonel became a little simple. Every day he would go for a walk through the woods near his house and greet everything he saw, saying, "Hullo, tree; hullo, birdies; hullo, flowers."

One day he went further into the woods than he had ever done before, and discovered a little black ebony idol.

"Hullo, little black ebony idol," he said.

"Hello, Colonel," the idol replied. "Will you help me? I am not really a black ebony idol, but a beautiful girl. A wicked witch put me under a spell many years ago and all I need to release me is to have sexual intercourse with a presentable man."

"Well, I'd like to help you out," said the Colonel, "but I'm afraid I'm a bit past it. There's nothing I can do."

"Oh, Colonel," said the little black ebony idol, "you've got to help me. It may be years before another man comes along."

"Don't worry about it," said the Colonel. "I can't do anything for you myself, but I'll talk to my footman. He's an idle fucking bastard."

The Colonel's condition was very weak. He lay propped up in bed in the hospital, fed by tubes and injections, and surrounded by his loving family who carried on a strained conversation with him through the oxygen tent that enclosed him.

His first son asked him, "Are you comfortable, Father?"

"Yes, thanks."

"Are they looking after you all right?"

"Yes, thanks."

"Is there anything we can do for you?"

"Yes. Take your goddam foot off the oxygen hose."

When at last the Colonel passed away and was about to be laid to rest, her ladyship received an unexpected visit from two solemn representatives from the funeral directors. They had run into a slight difficulty. It seemed that the corpse had had an erection and they were unable to fasten the lid on the coffin.

"We were wondering if your ladyship would mind if we cut it off and laid it beside him with the flowers.

Her ladyship thought about this for a moment, then replied, "Yes. I suppose that would be all right. Although, on second thoughts, it might be better if you cut it off and shoved it up his arse. That's what he used to do to me when I had the flowers."